Matt Hazard

Return
of the Naive

kieltyascharged

Fair Acre Press

First published by Fair Acre Press in 2018
www.fairacrepress.co.uk

A CIP catalogue record for this book is available from the British Library

ISBN 978-1-911048-31-2

Printed and bound by Lightning Source

Lightning Source has received Chain of Custody (CoC) certification from:
The Forest Stewardship CouncilTM (FSC®)
Programme for the Endorsement of Forest CertificationTM (PEFCTM) The Sustainable Forestry Initiative® (SFI®)

Cover Images by Paul Kielty
Typeset and Cover Design by Nadia Kingsley

Meet Matt Hazard.
An ordinary guy that's trying not to be defined by his job.

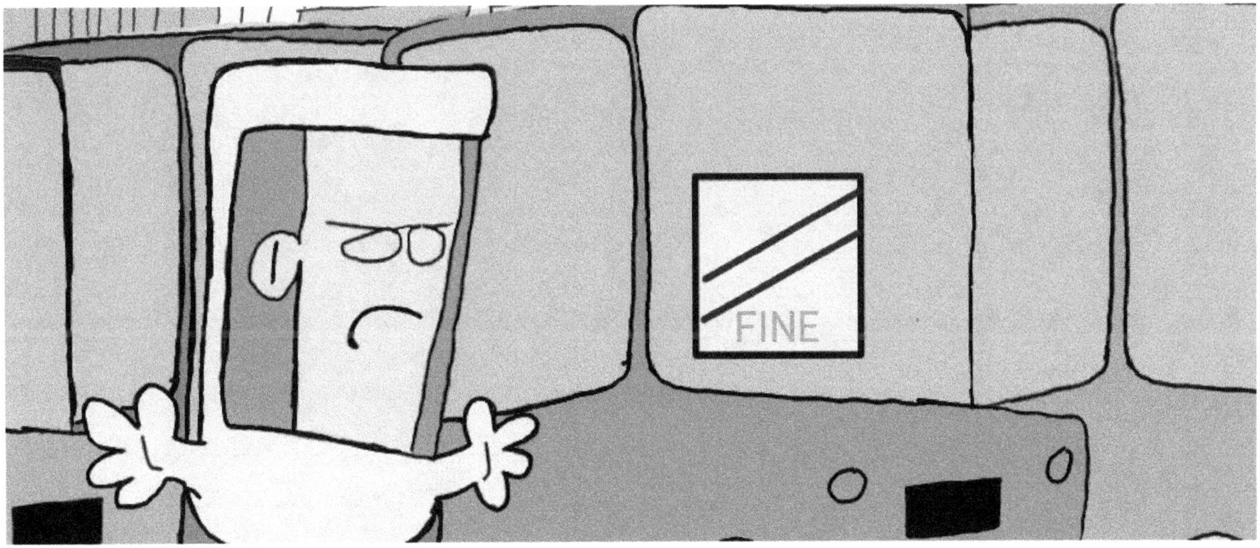
FINE

This is for all the Matt Hazards out there. Like me.
And for my brother Brendan
the eejit that he is.

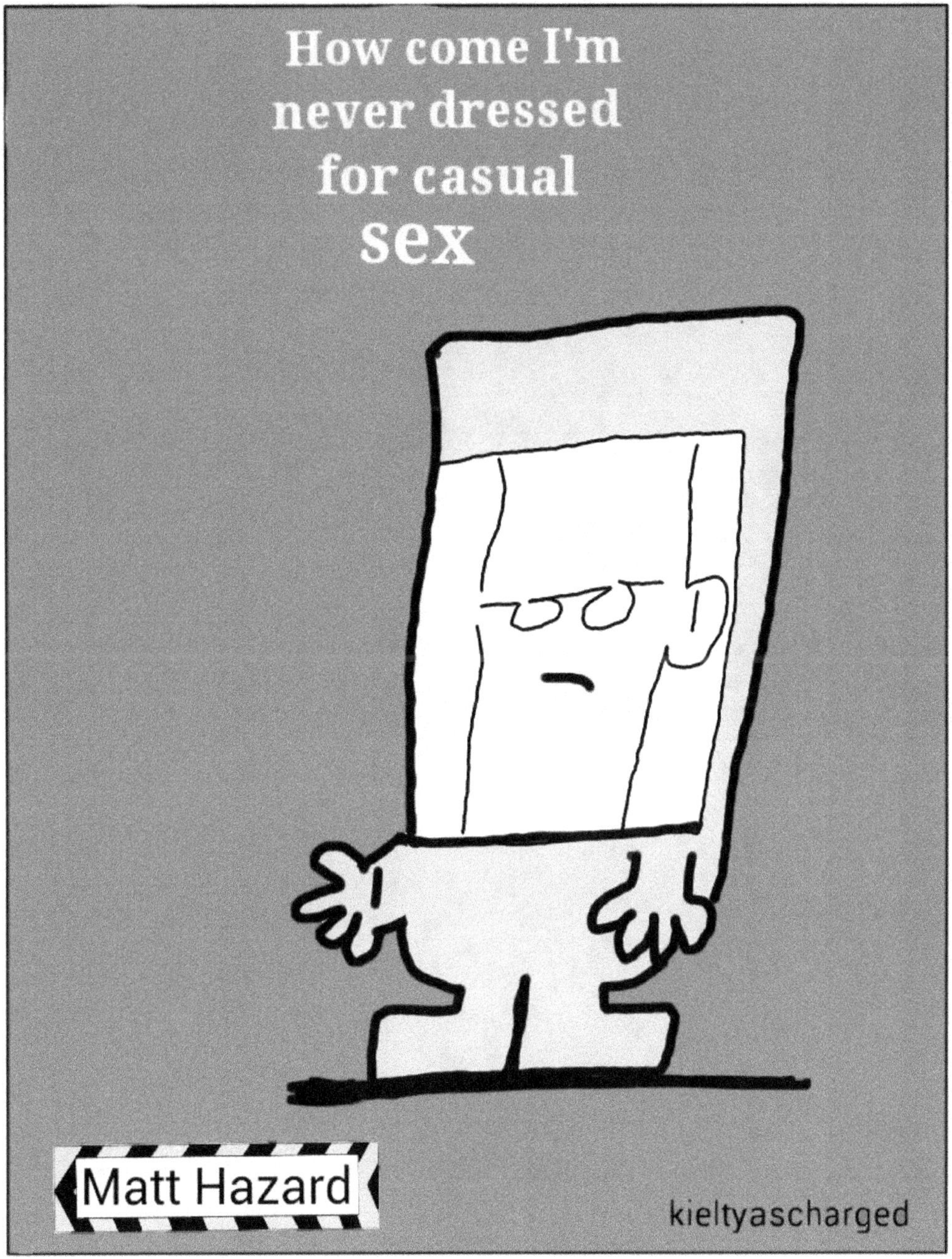
How come I'm
never dressed
for casual
sex
Matt Hazard
kieltyascharged

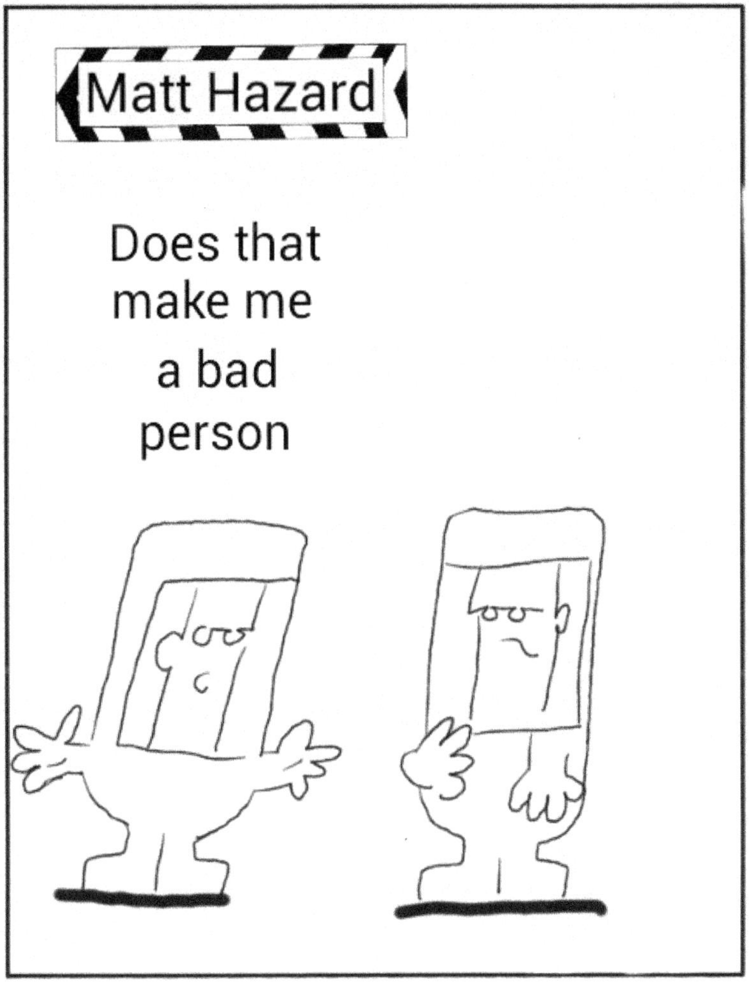
Matt Hazard
Does that make me a bad person

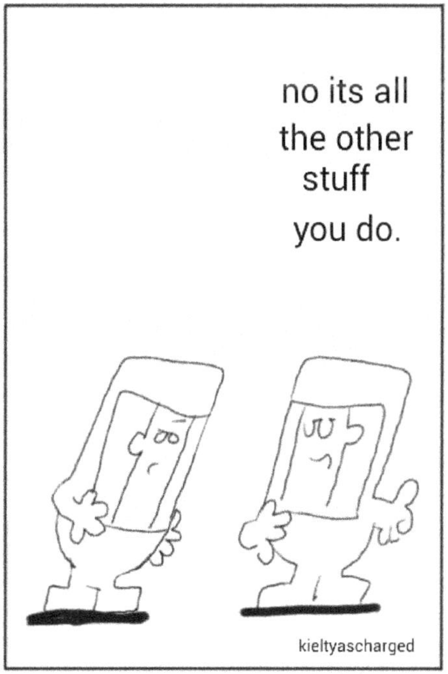
no its all the other stuff you do.
kieltyascharged

Matt Hazard

This was an expensive holiday even the tumble weed had roaming charges.

kieltyascharged

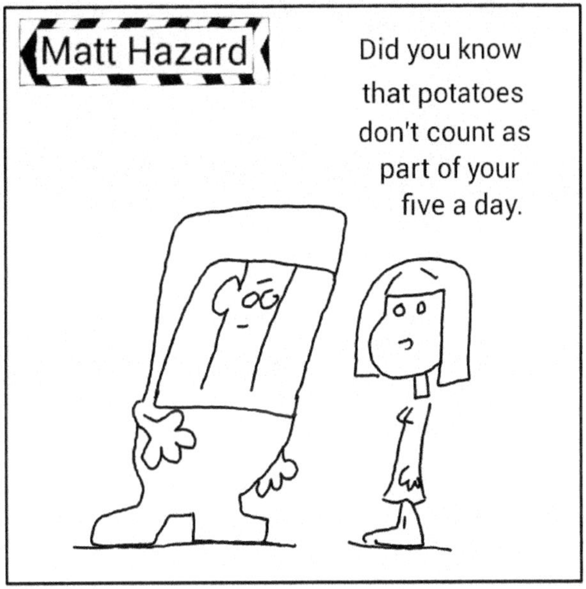
Matt Hazard
Did you know that potatoes don't count as part of your five a day.

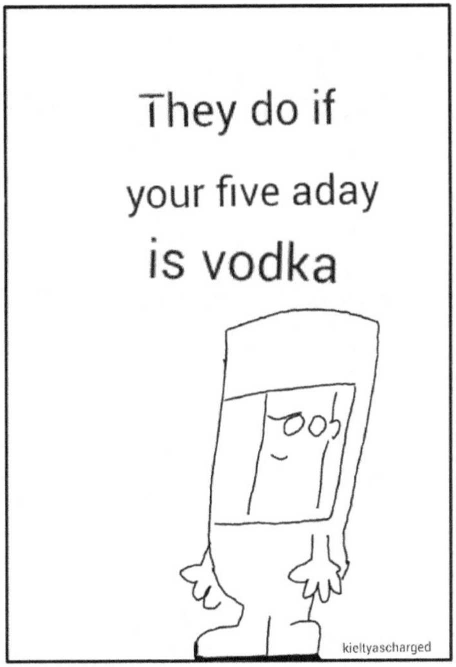
They do if your five aday is vodka
kieltyascharged

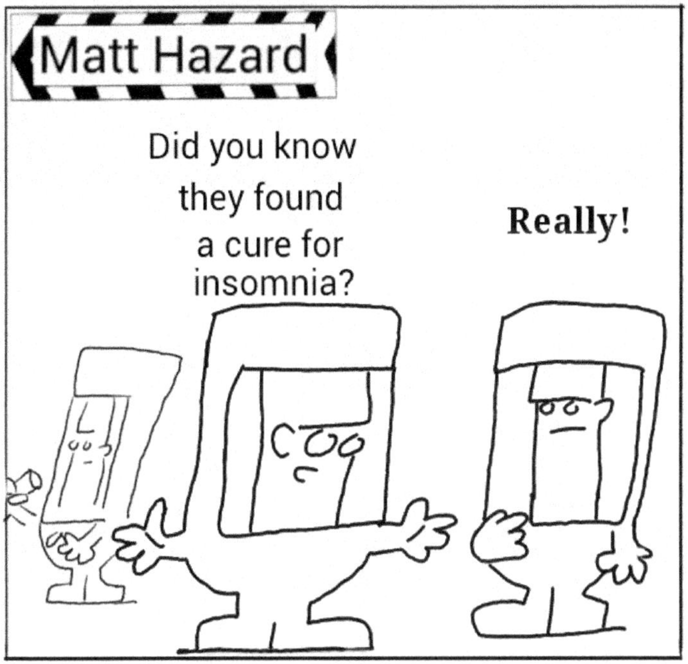
Matt Hazard
Did you know they found a cure for insomnia?
Really!

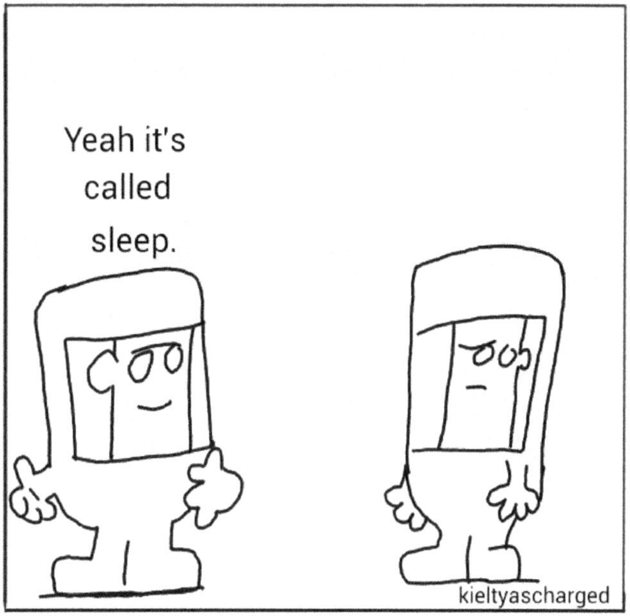
Yeah it's called sleep.
kieltyascharged

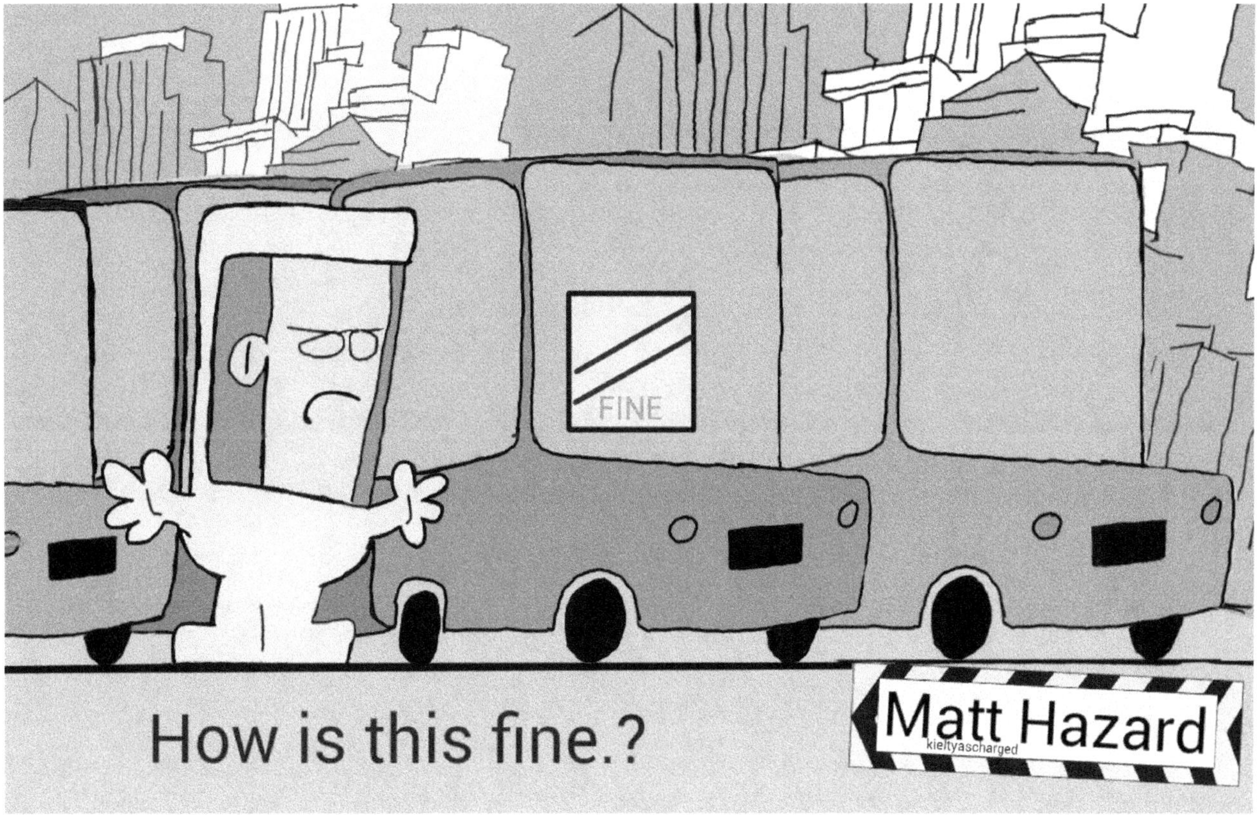
FINE
How is this fine.?
Matt Hazard
kieltyascharged

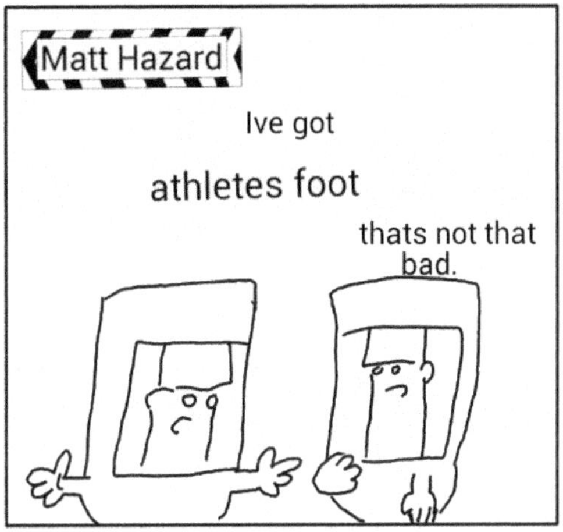
Matt Hazard
Ive got
athletes foot
thats not that bad.

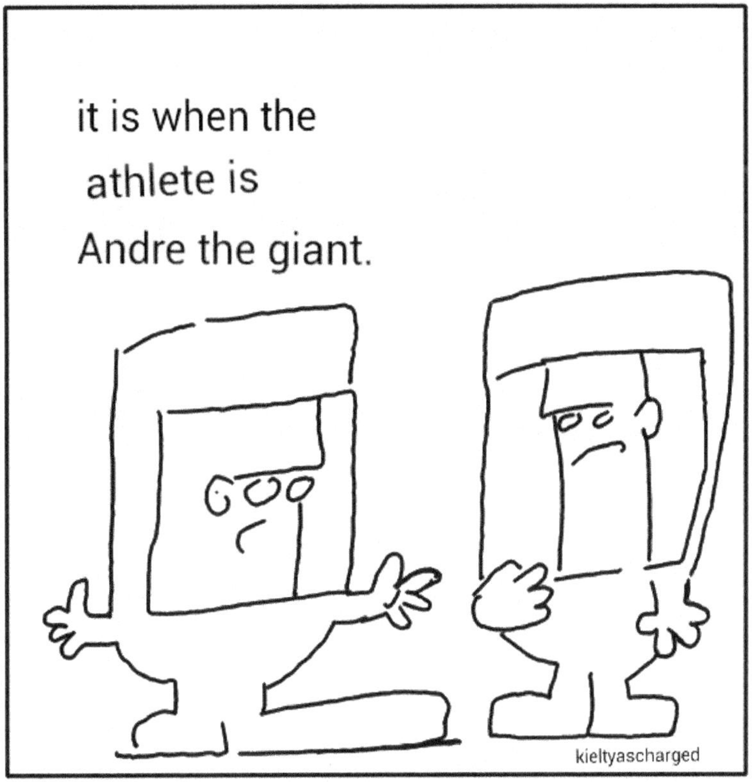
it is when the
athlete is
Andre the giant.
kieltyascharged

what do you
mean my bathing suit
is offensive?

contains nuts

Matt Hazard

kieltyascharged

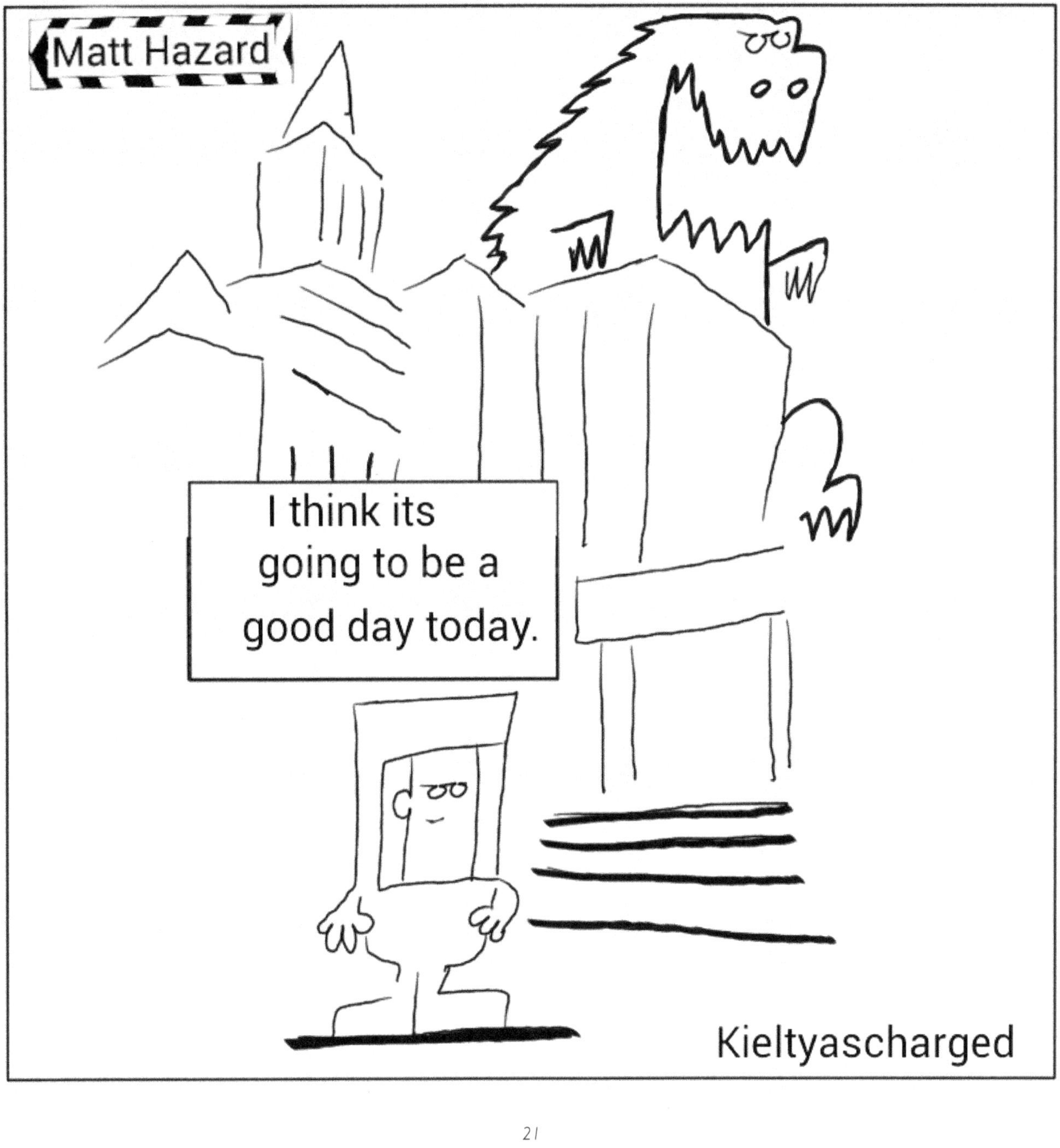
Matt Hazard
I think its going to be a good day today.
Kieltyascharged

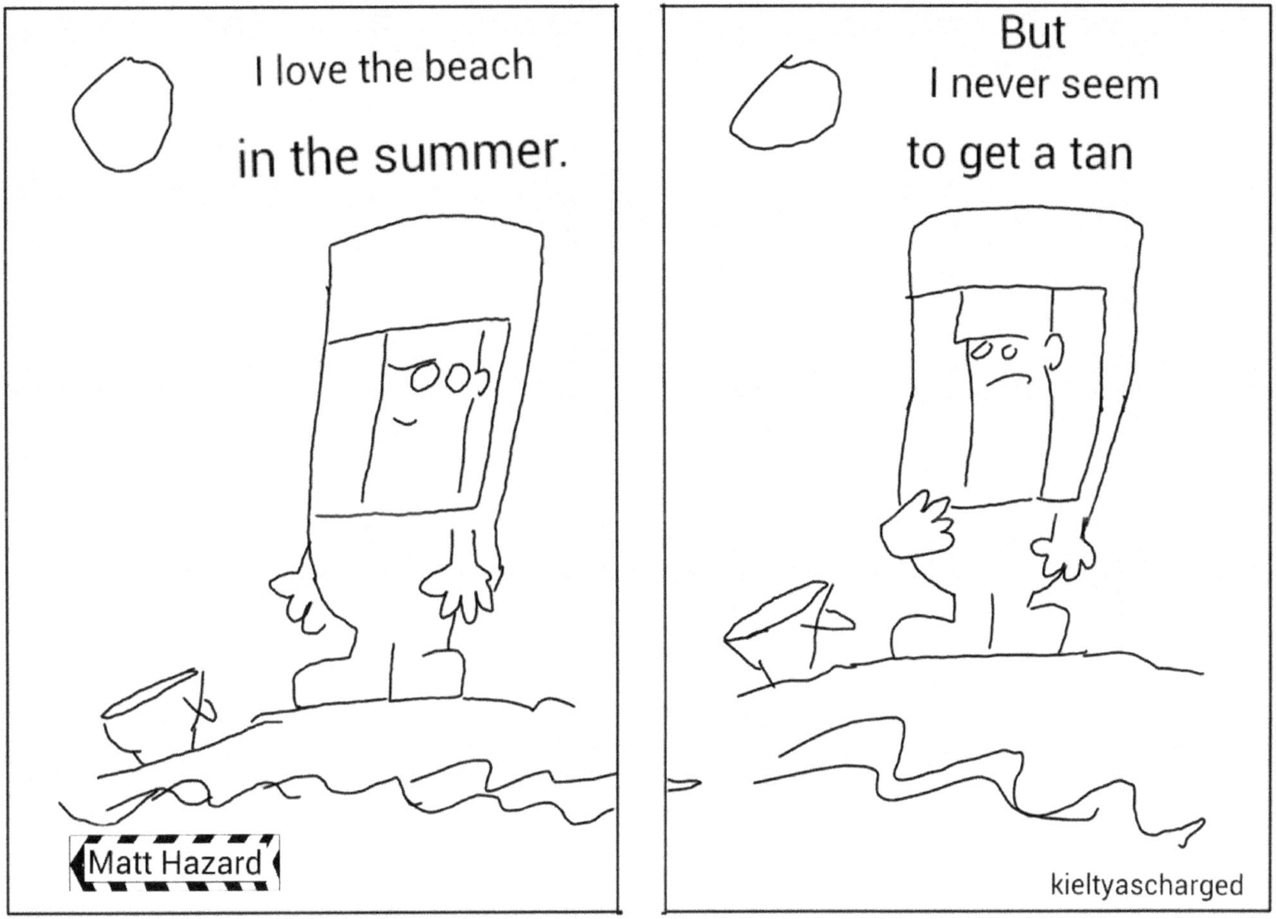
I love the beach
in the summer.
Matt Hazard
But
I never seem
to get a tan
kieltyascharged

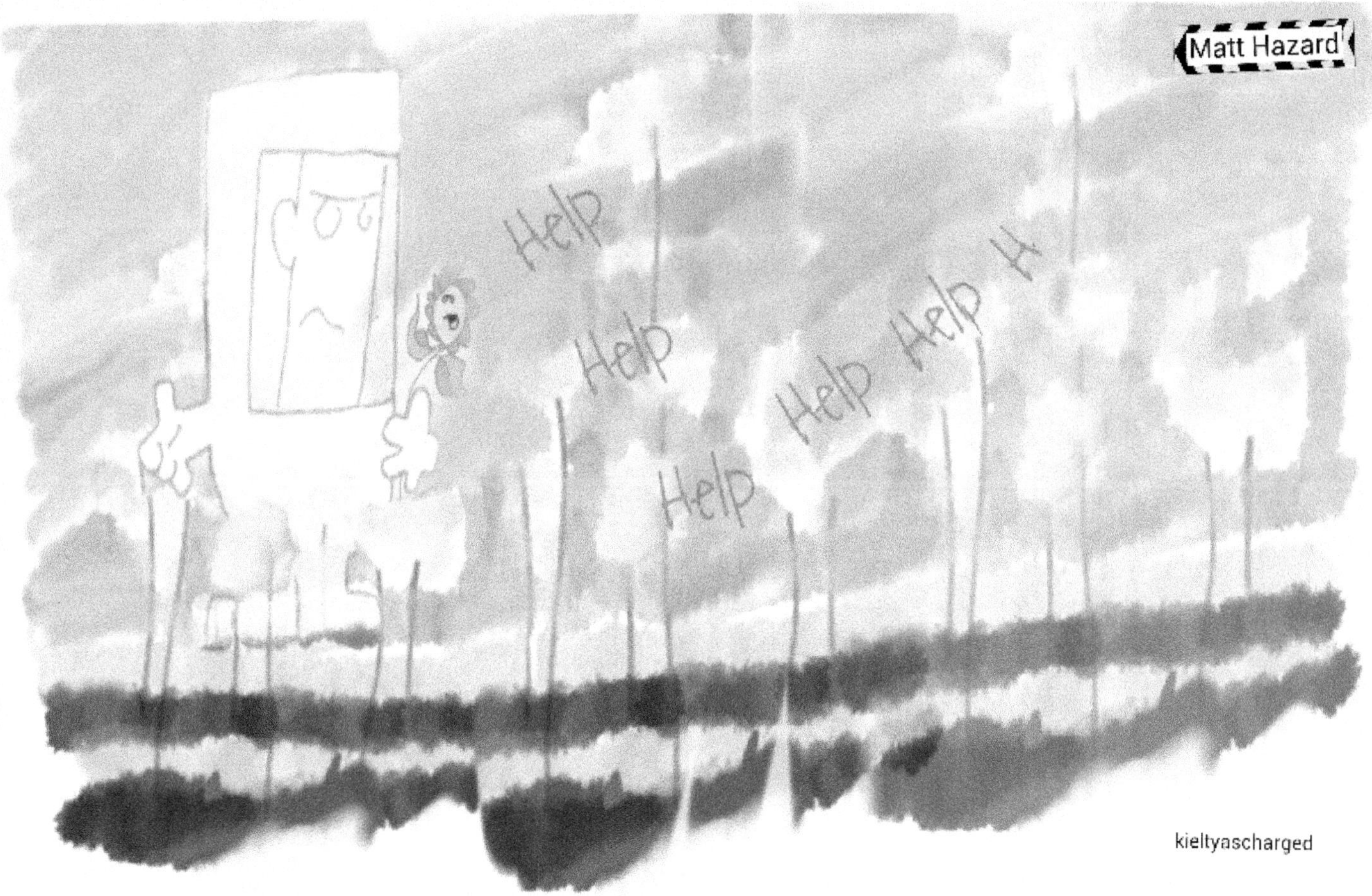
Matt Hazard
Help
Help
Help Help H
Help
Help
kieltyascharged

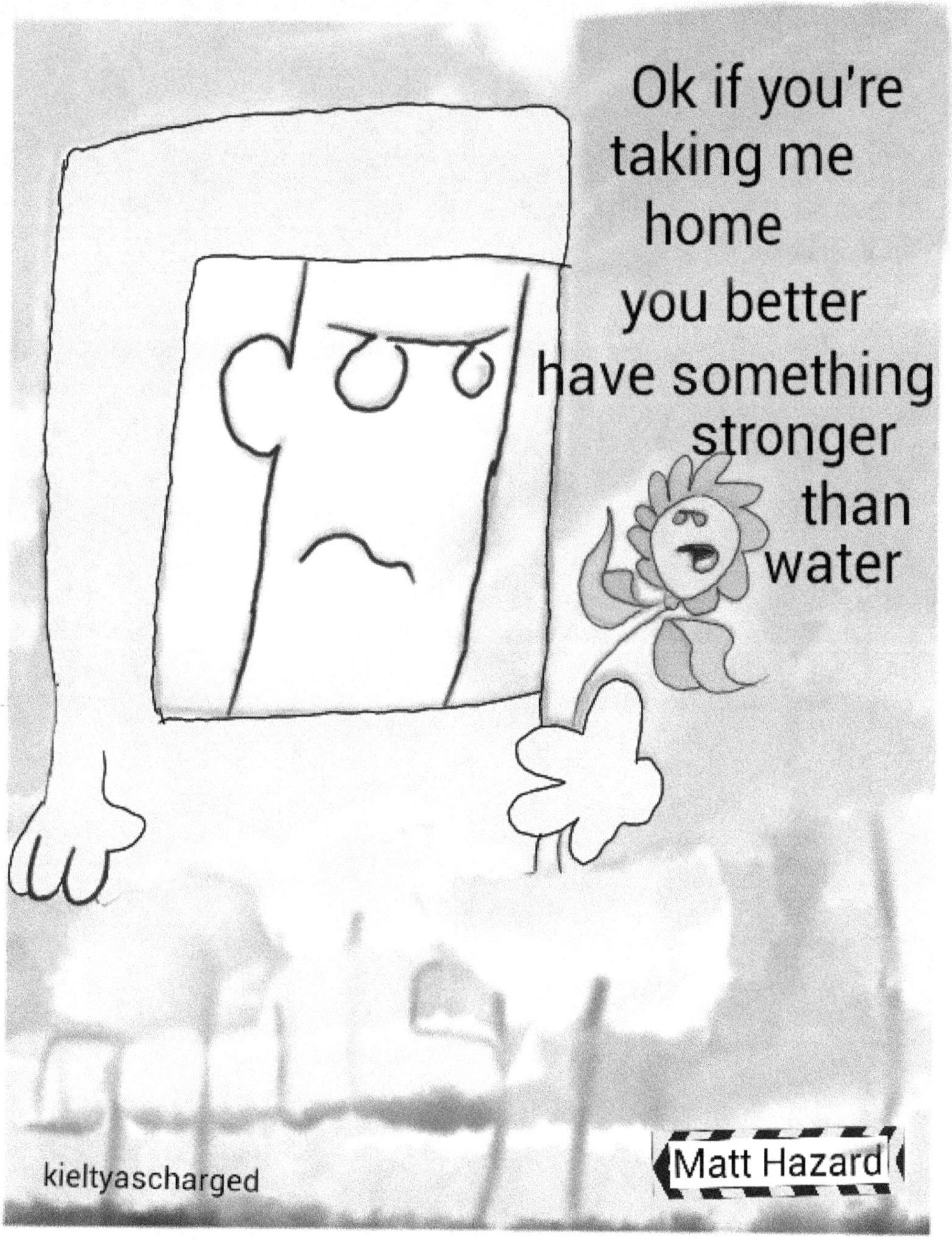
Ok if you're taking me home you better have something stronger than water
kieltyascharged
Matt Hazard

Matt Hazard

Look signs
of early man.

How do you
know it was
early man

I looked
at my
watch

kieltyascharged

29

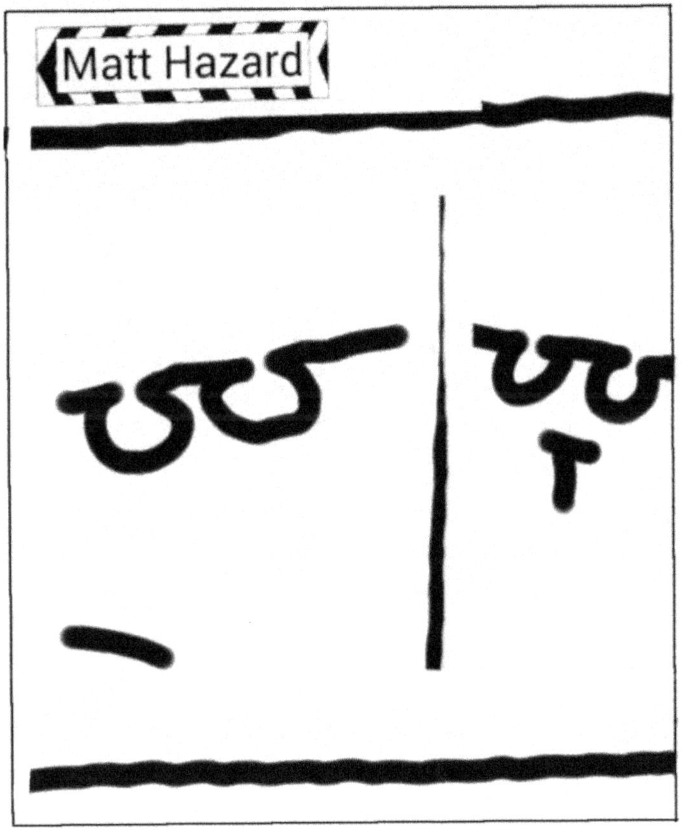
Matt Hazard

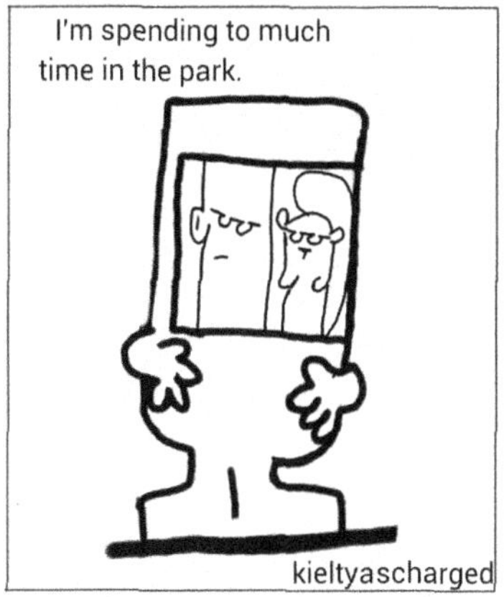
I'm spending to much
time in the park.
kieltyascharged

Matt Hazard

You'd better not be thinking about nuts.

kieltyascharged

33

Matt Hazard

One of us

has got

to go.

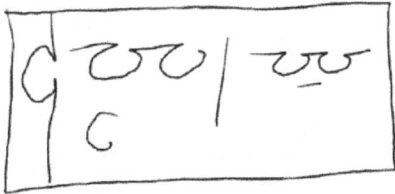

I thought he'd

never leave.

kieltyascharged

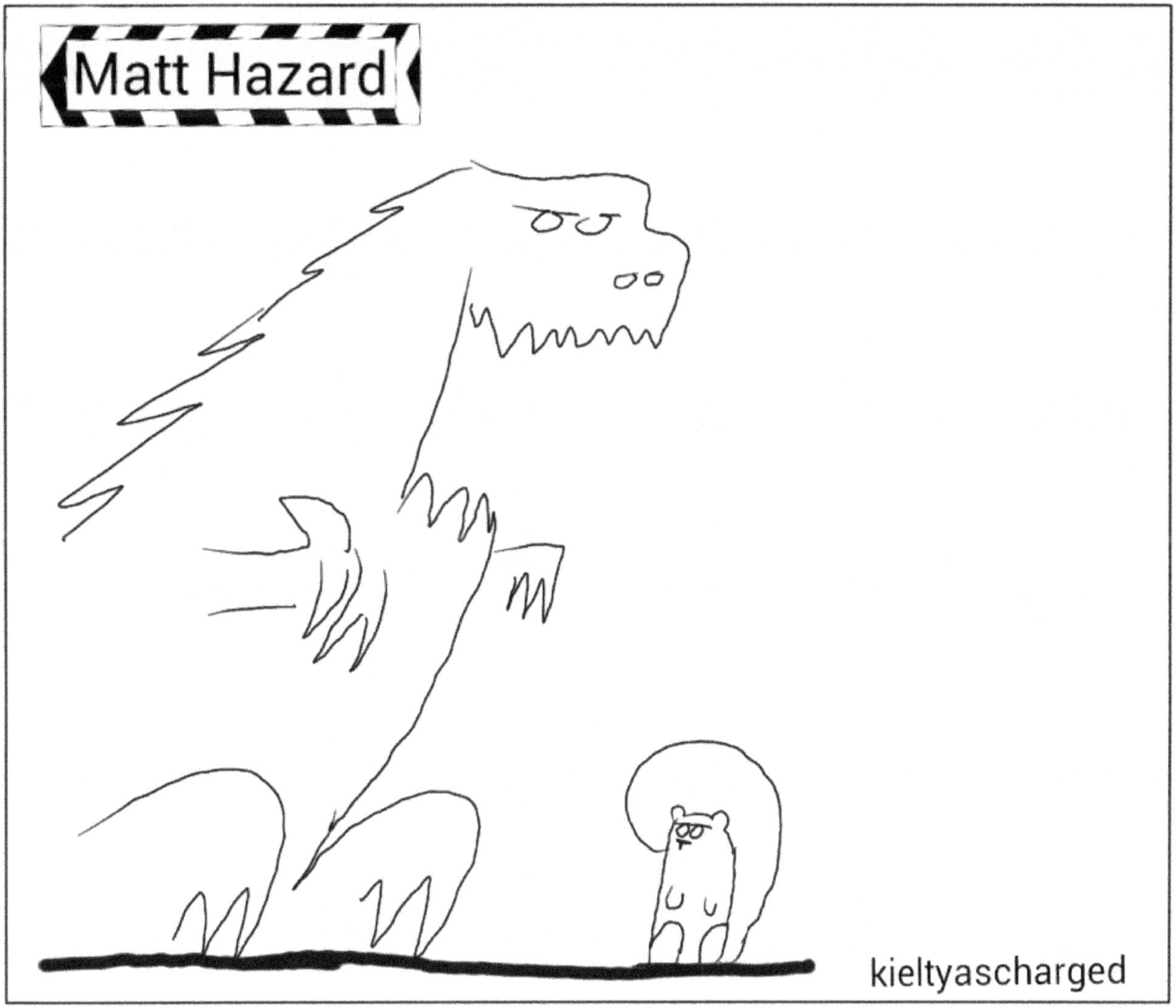
Matt Hazard
kieltyascharged

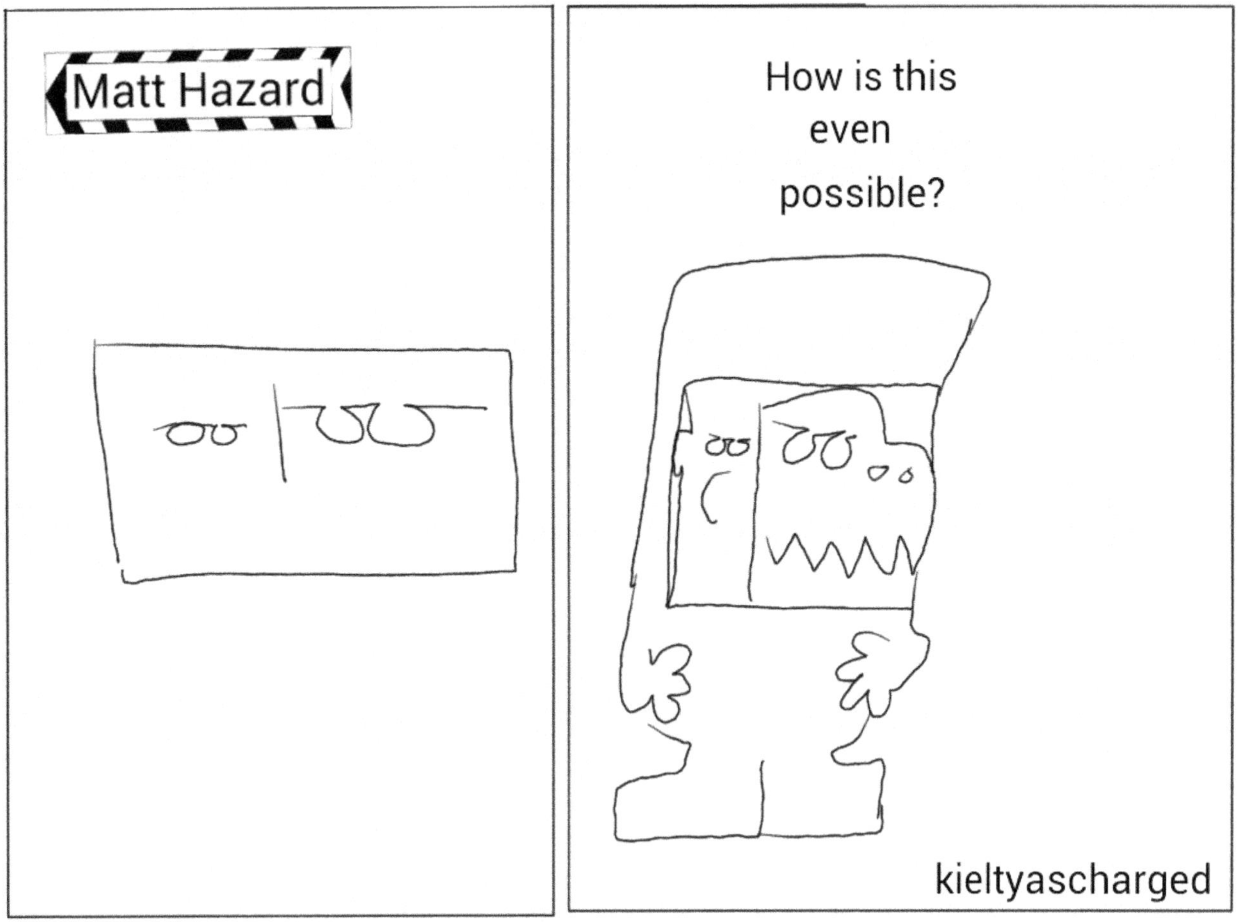
Matt Hazard
How is this even possible?
kieltyascharged

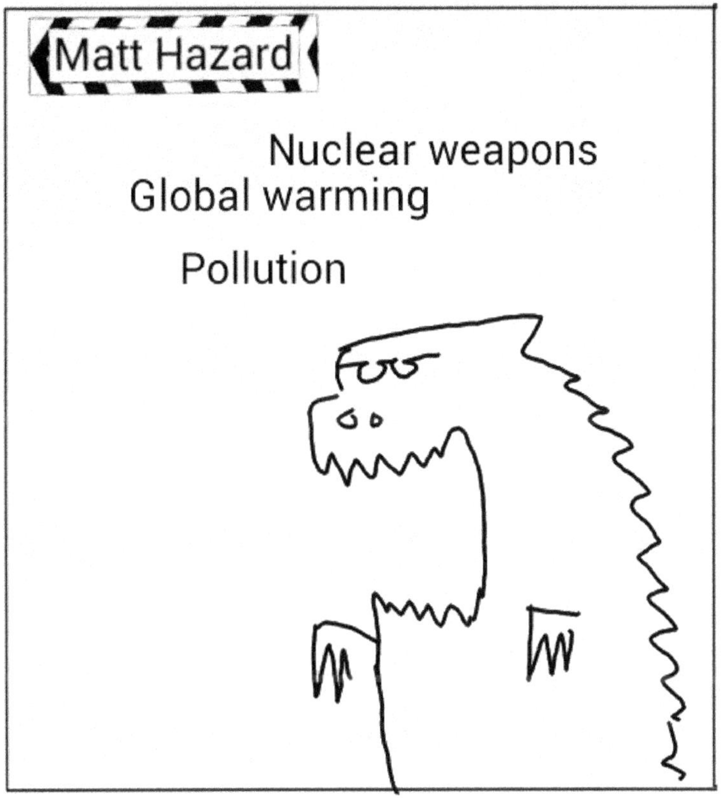
Matt Hazard
Nuclear weapons
Global warming
Pollution

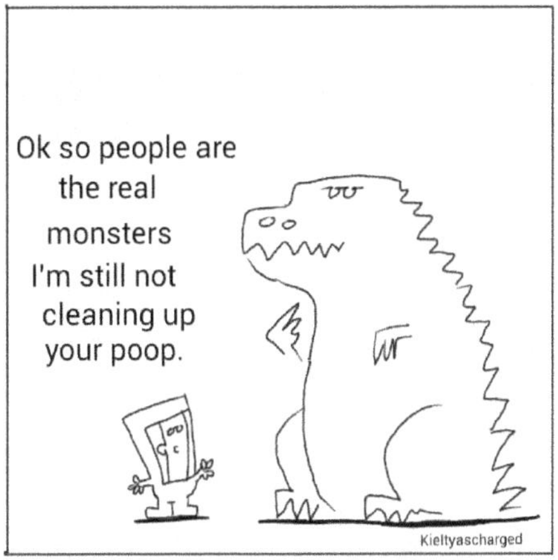
Ok so people are the real monsters I'm still not cleaning up your poop.
Kieltyascharged

Matt Hazard

what ya mean oh no
an ALIEN
I don't see your name
on any film franchise

kieltyascharged

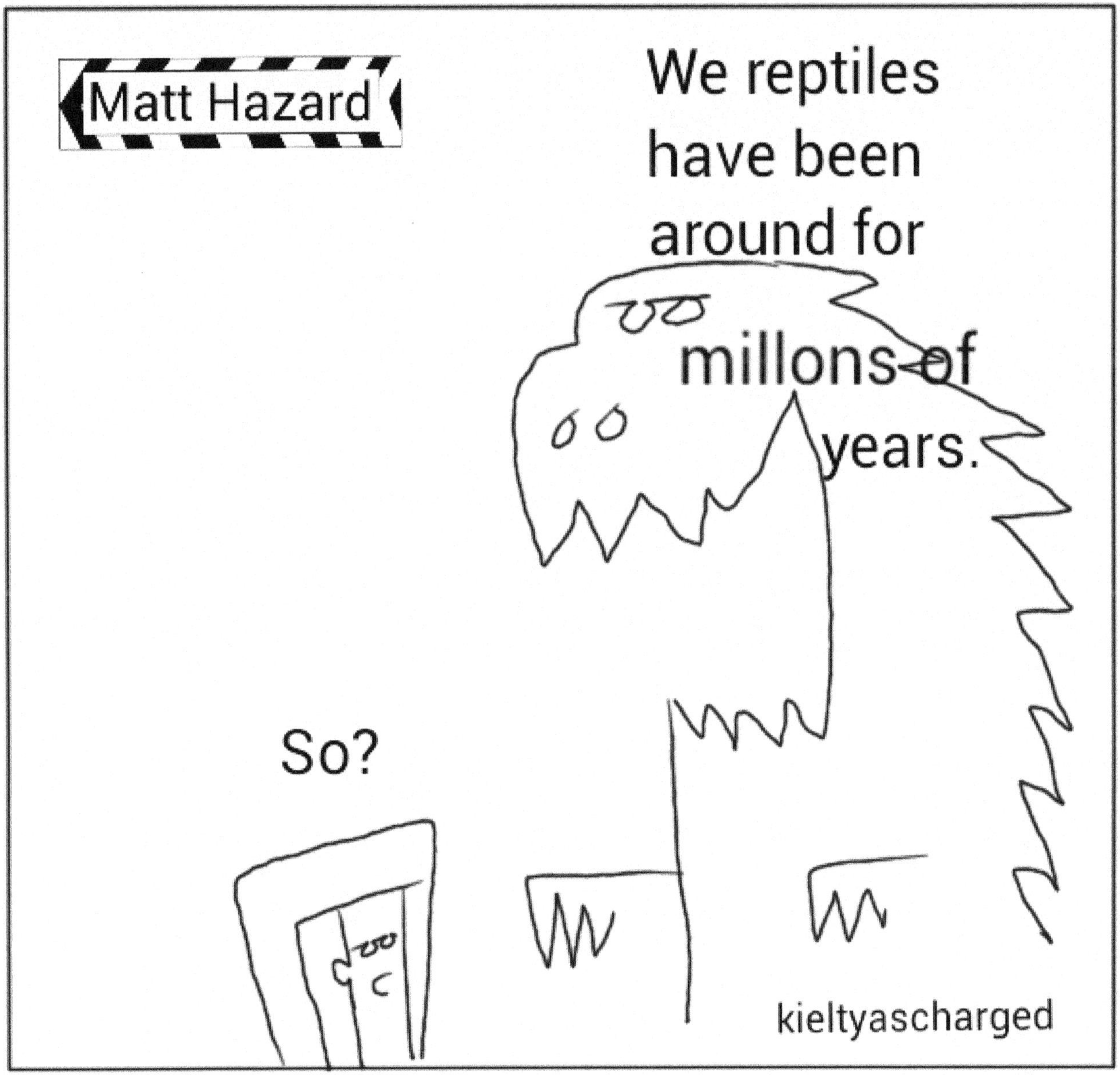
Matt Hazard
We reptiles have been around for millons of years.
So?
kieltyascharged

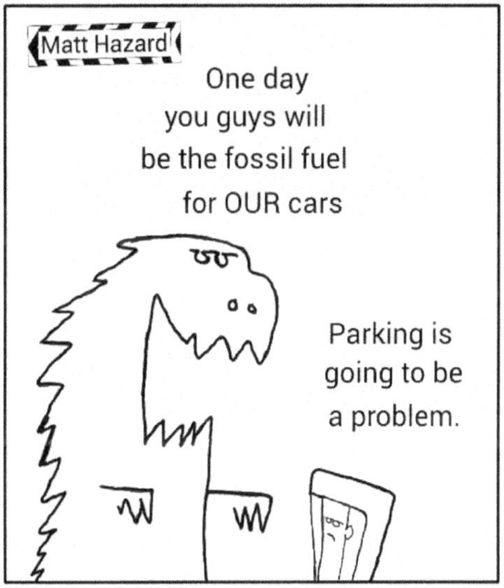
Matt Hazard
One day you guys will be the fossil fuel for OUR cars
Parking is going to be a problem.

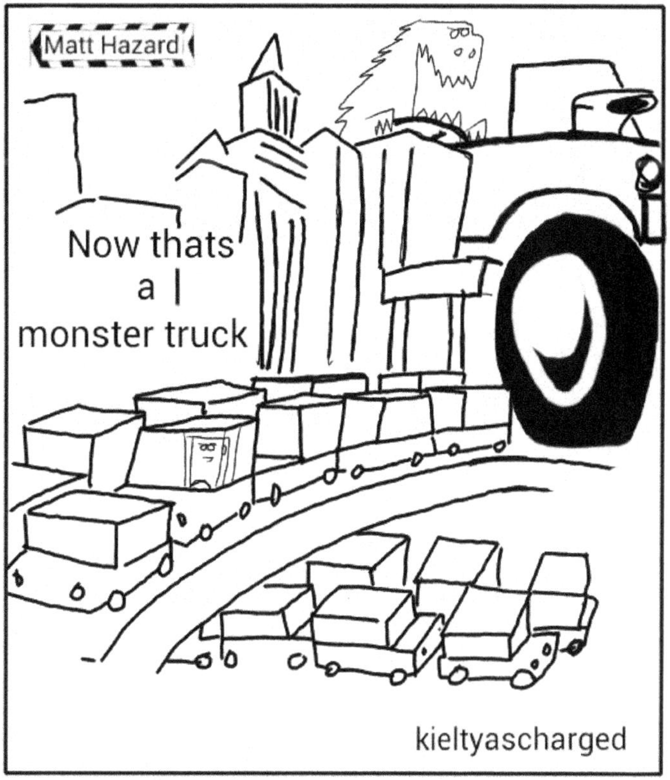
Matt Hazard
Now thats a monster truck
kieltyascharged

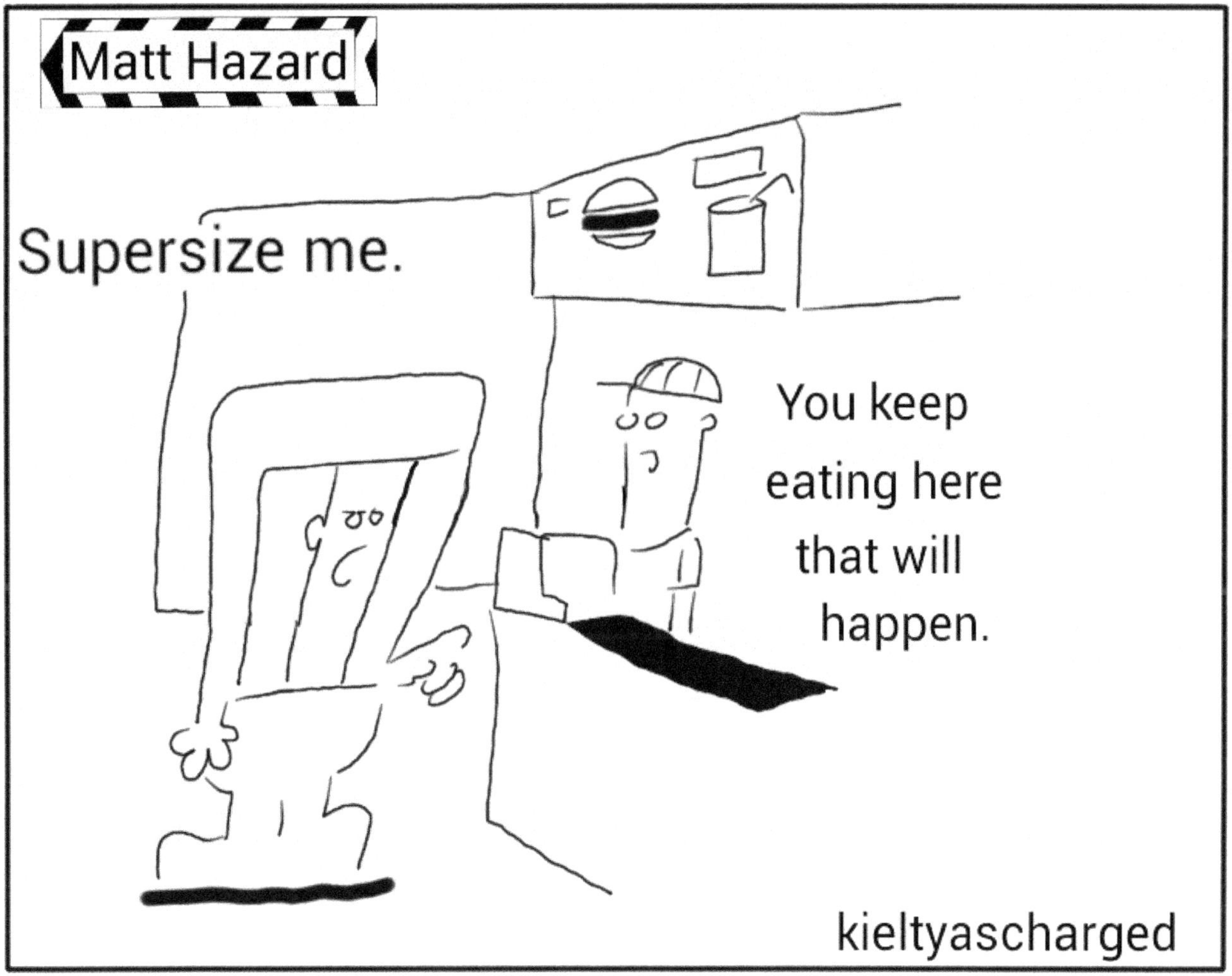
Matt Hazard
Supersize me.
You keep eating here that will happen.
kieltyascharged

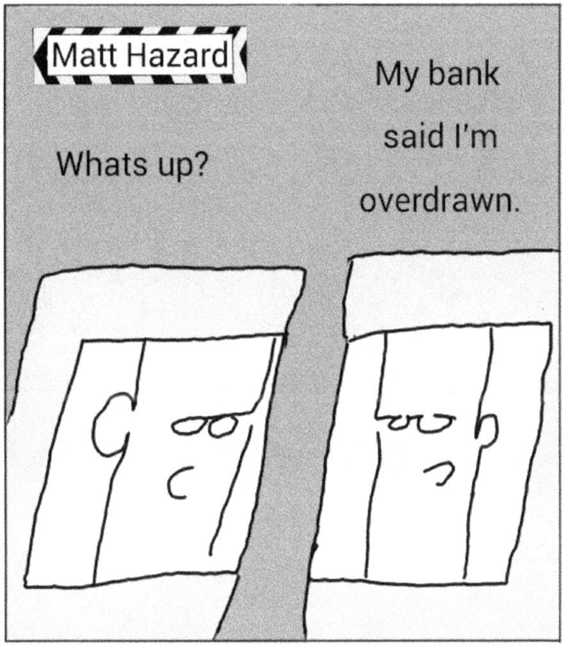
Matt Hazard
Whats up?
My bank said I'm overdrawn.

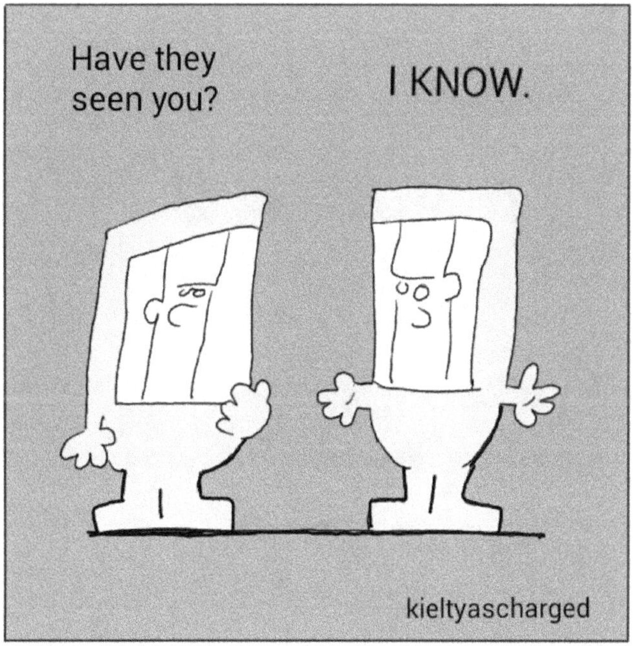
Have they seen you?
I KNOW.
kieltyascharged

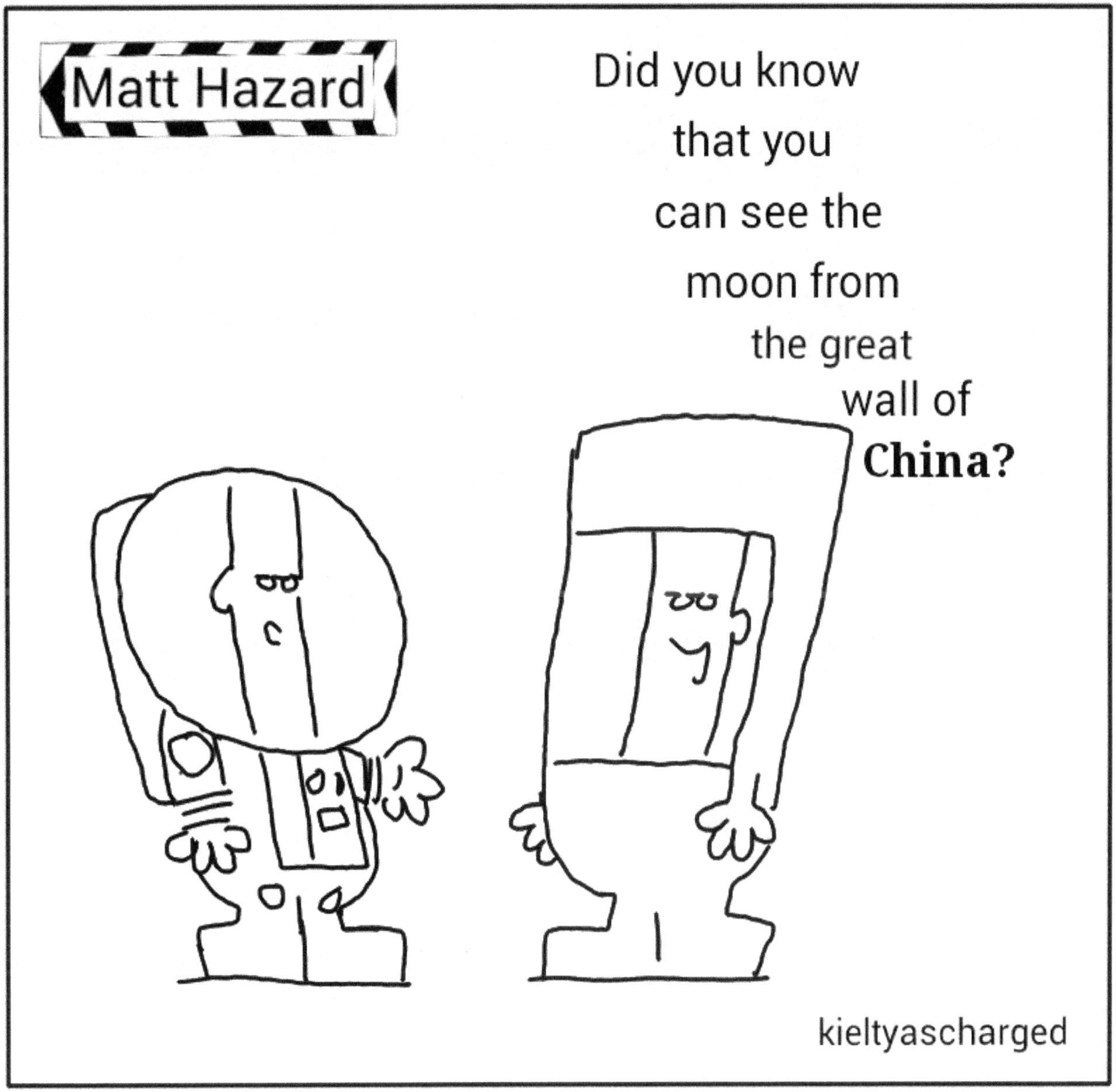
Matt Hazard
Did you know that you can see the moon from the great wall of **China?**
kieltyascharged

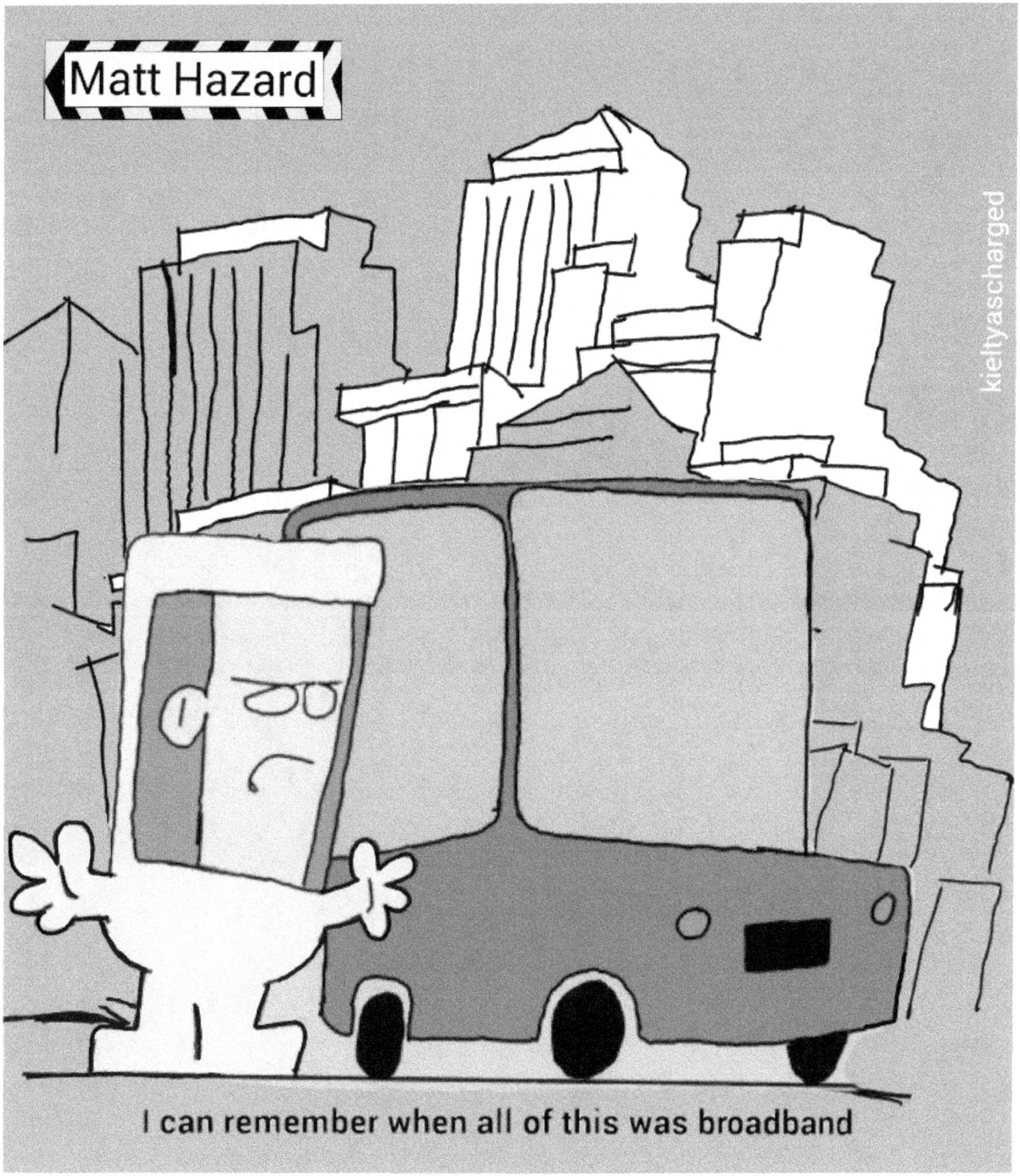
Matt Hazard
kieltyascharged
I can remember when all of this was broadband

Just to think that
life started here
in the very same sea
millions of years ago.

Matt Hazard

Great now everything smells like feet.

kieltyascharged

Matt Hazard
What's space like?
I don't know its pretty dark up there.
kieltyascharged

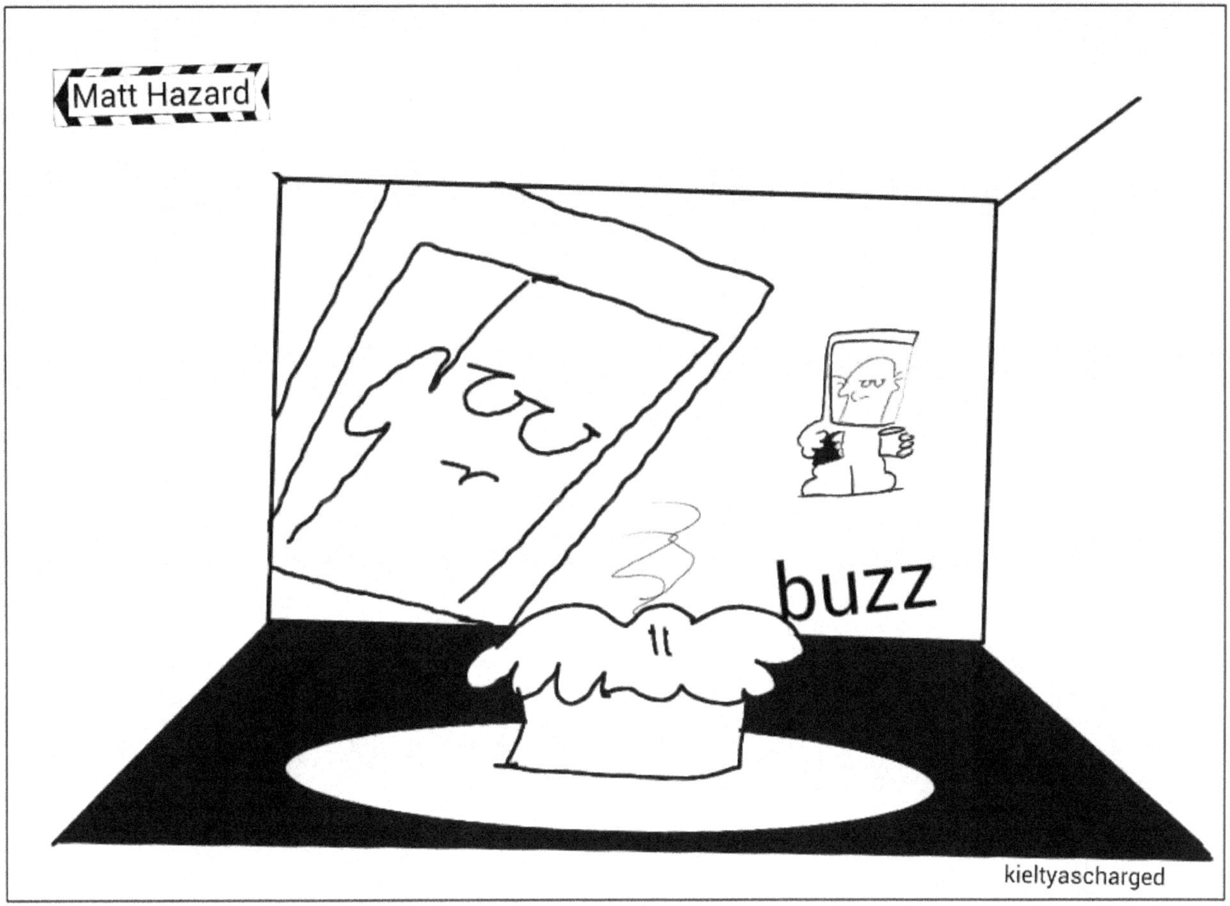
Matt Hazard
buzz
kieltyascharged

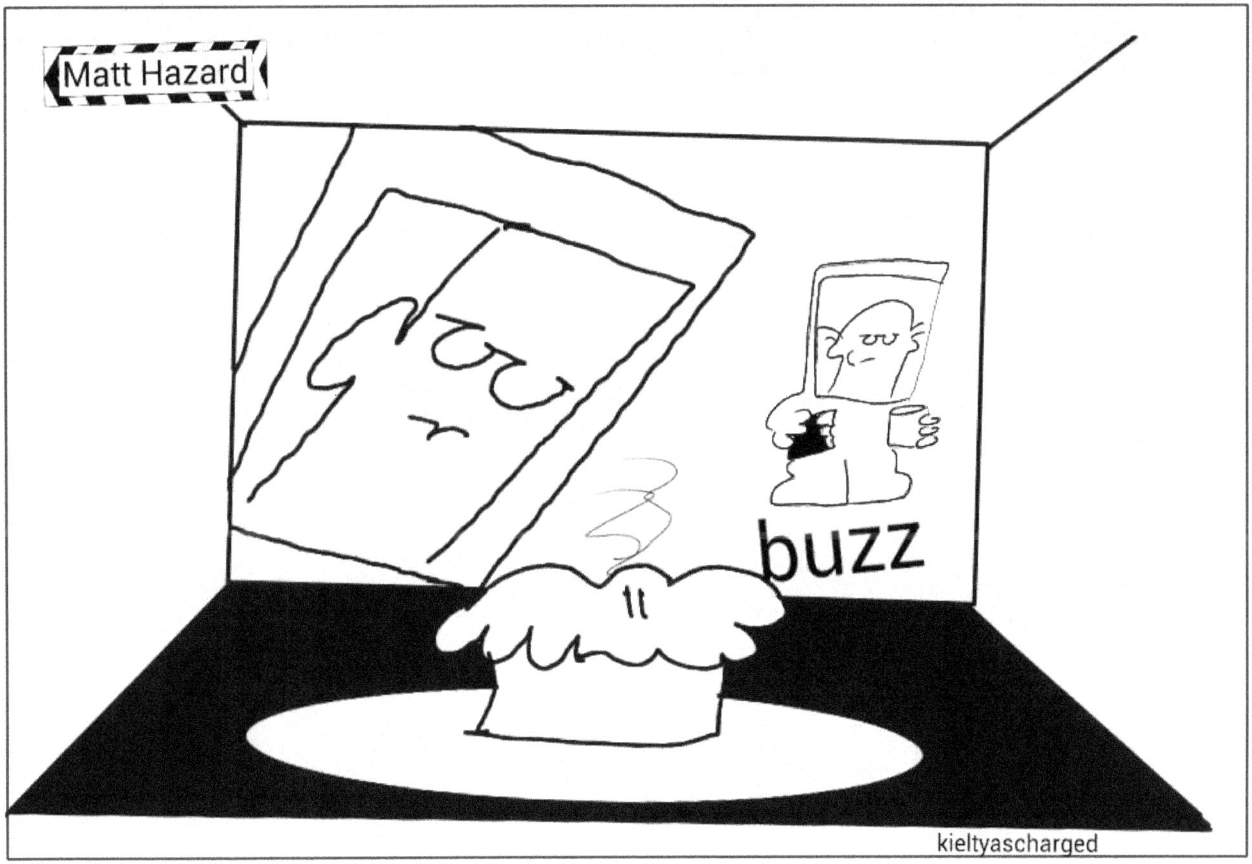
Matt Hazard
buzz
kieltyascharged

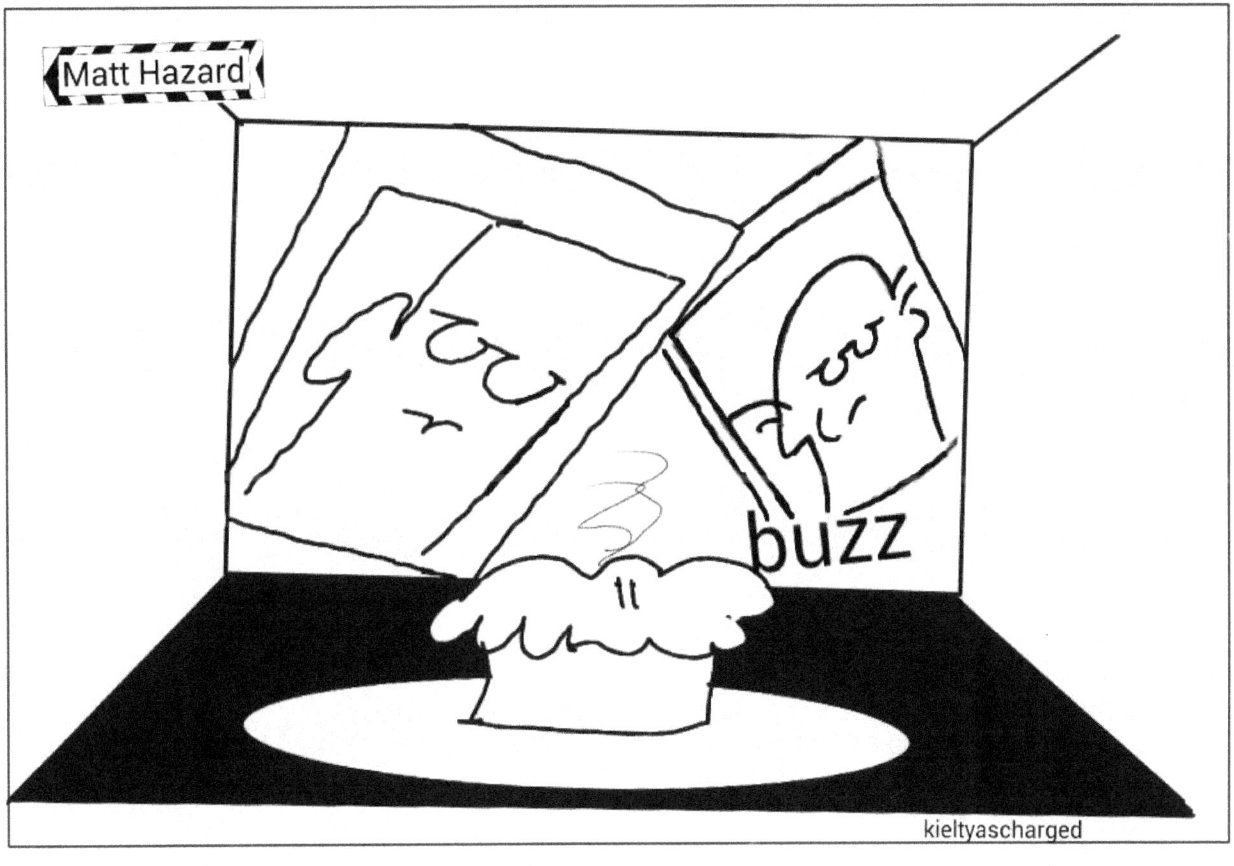
Matt Hazard
buzz
kieltyascharged

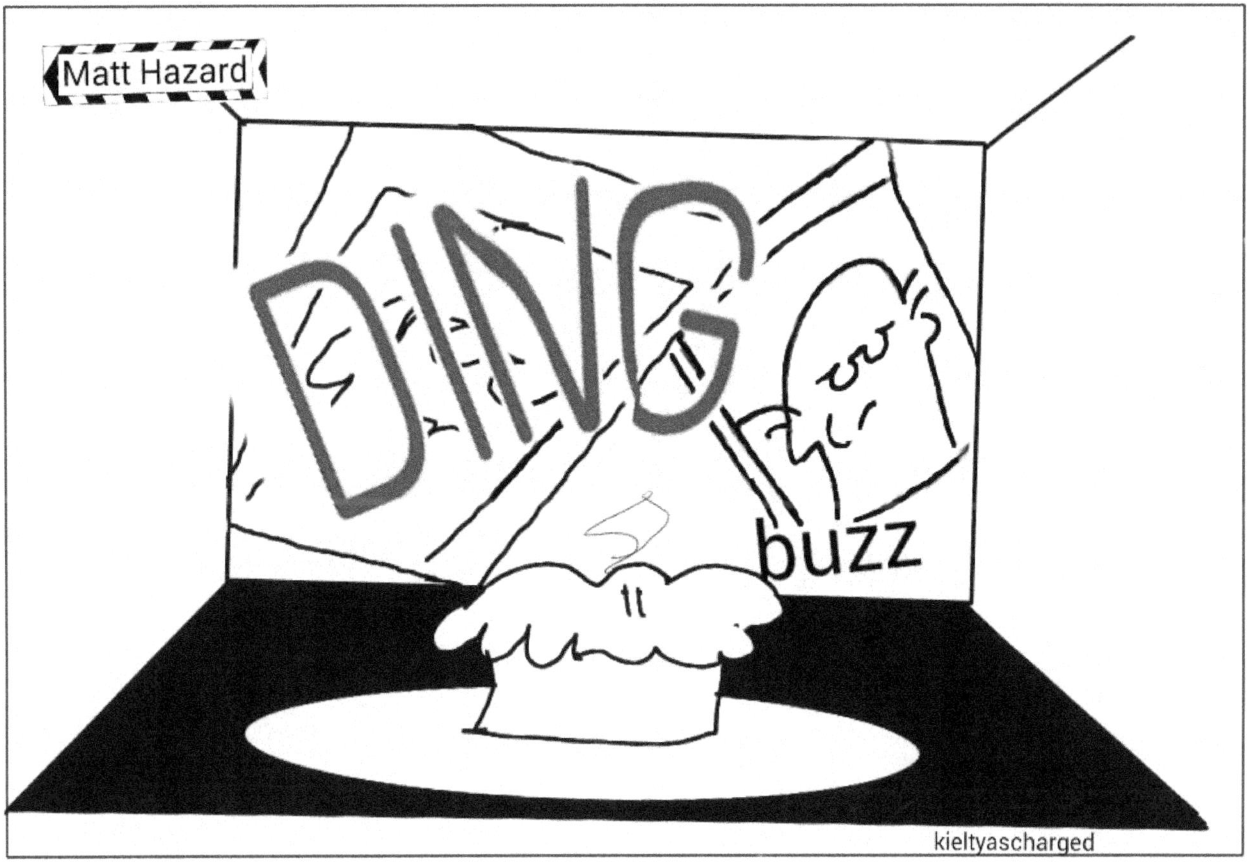
Matt Hazard
DING
buzz
kieltyascharged

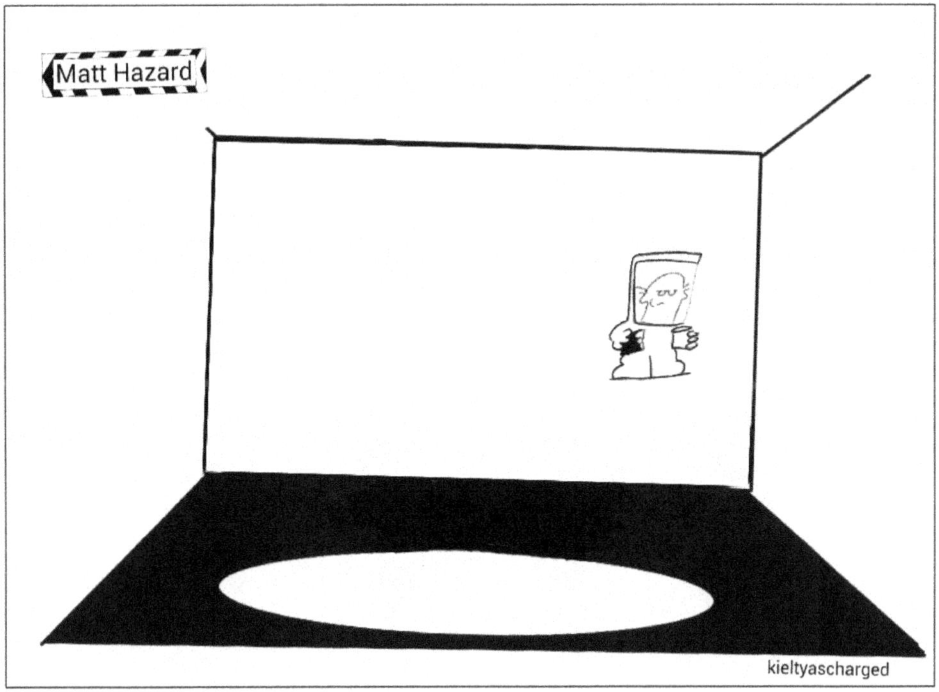
Matt Hazard
kieltyascharged

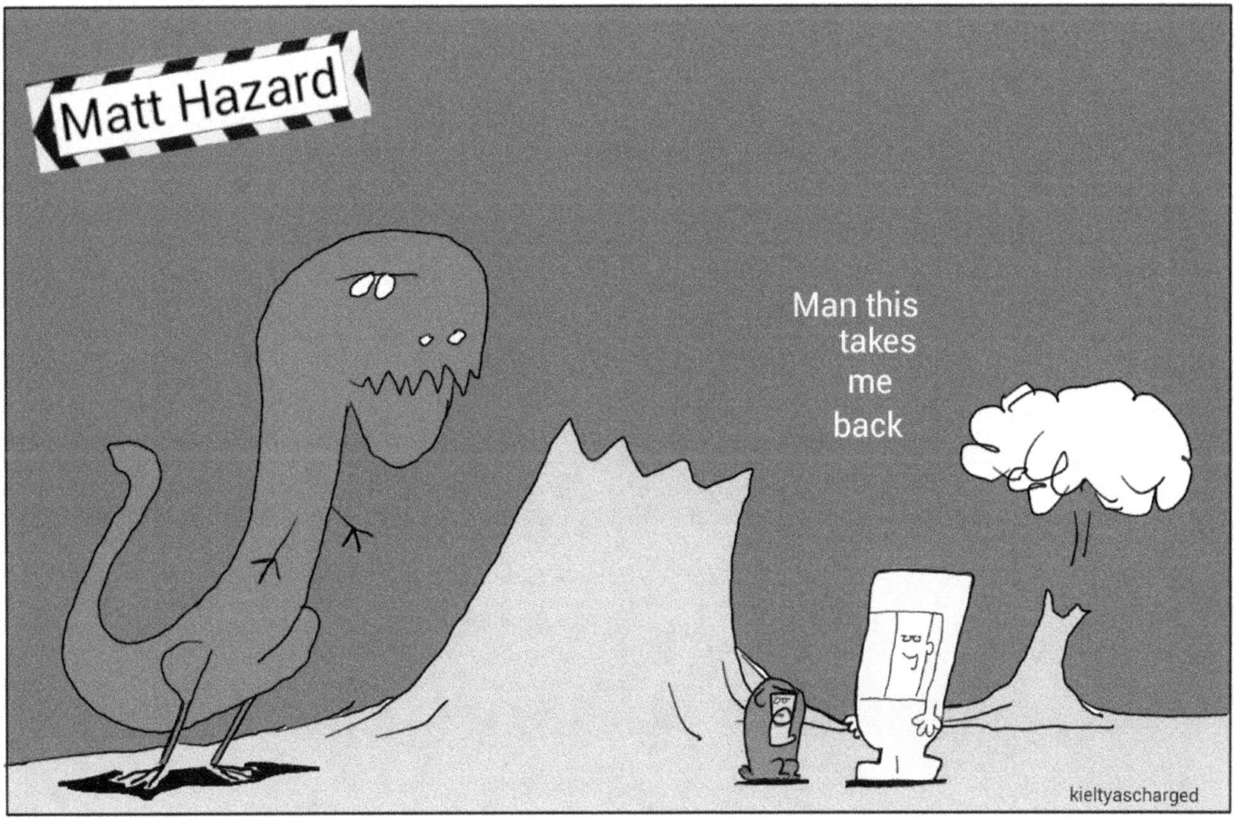
Matt Hazard
Man this takes me back
kieltyascharged

Matt Hazard
Hey did you know airplane tyres
are filled with helium
so they don't burst
at high altitude?
AIRPORT
kieltyascharged

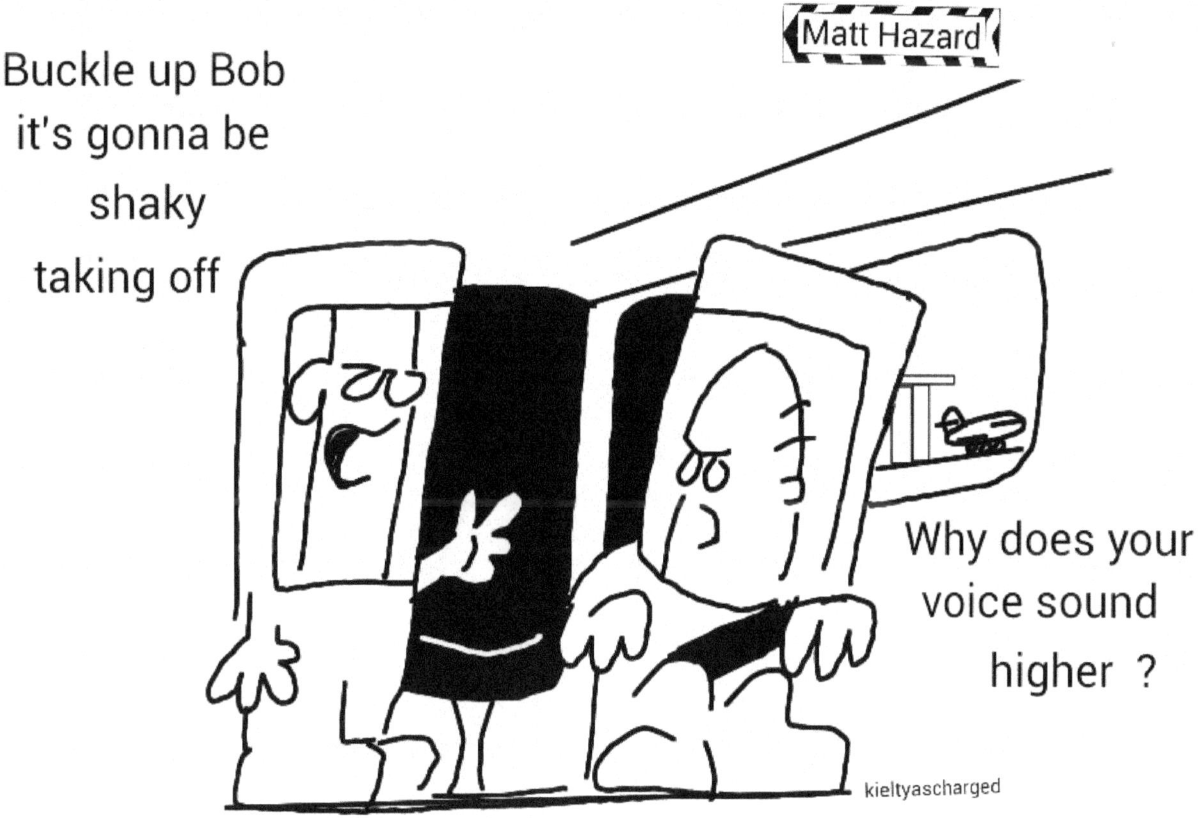
Buckle up Bob it's gonna be shaky taking off
Matt Hazard
Why does your voice sound higher ?
kieltyascharged

Matt Hazard
I'm not sure what a misogynist is
But if anything I'm a misterogynist
kieltyascharged

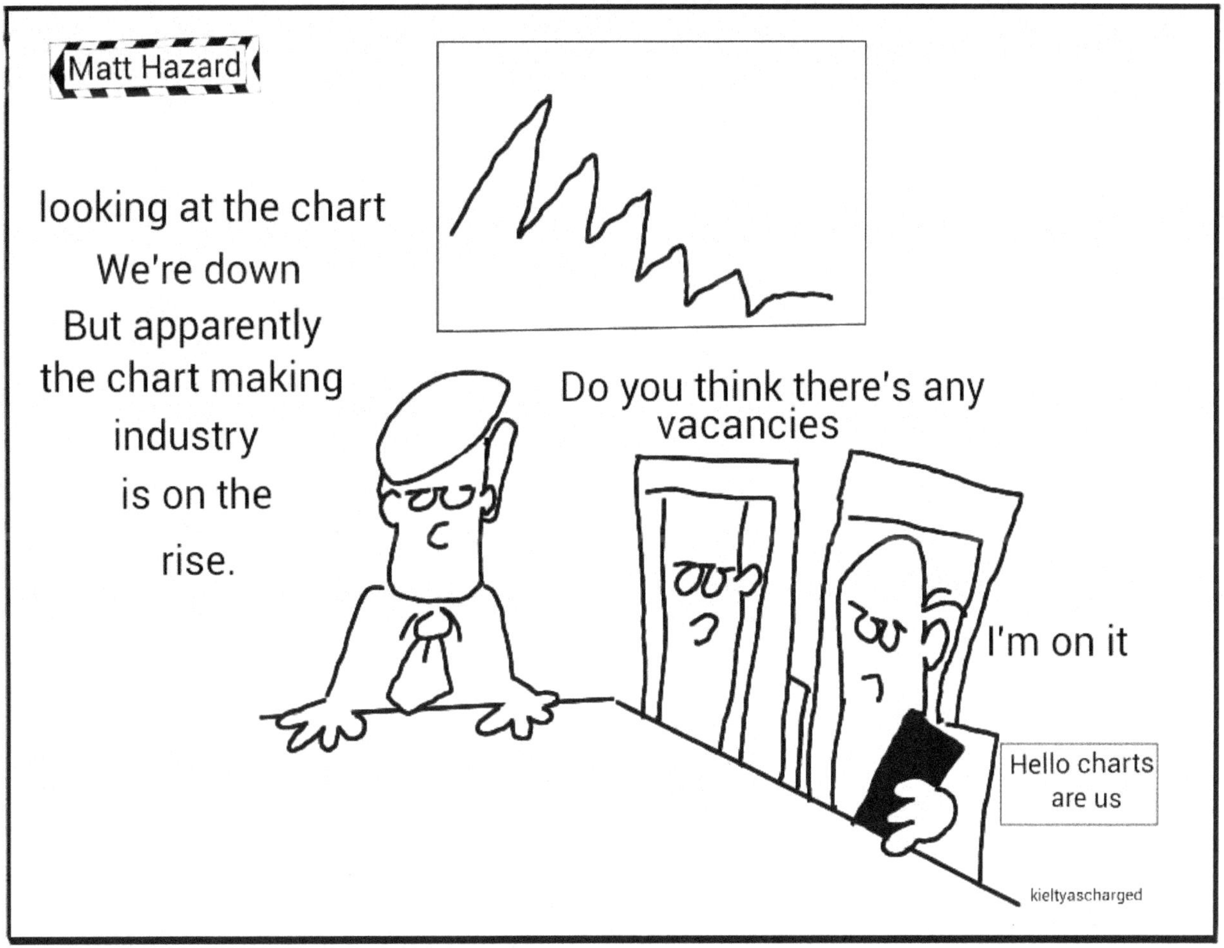
Matt Hazard
looking at the chart
We're down
But apparently
the chart making
industry
is on the
rise.
Do you think there's any
vacancies
I'm on it
Hello charts
are us
kieltyascharged

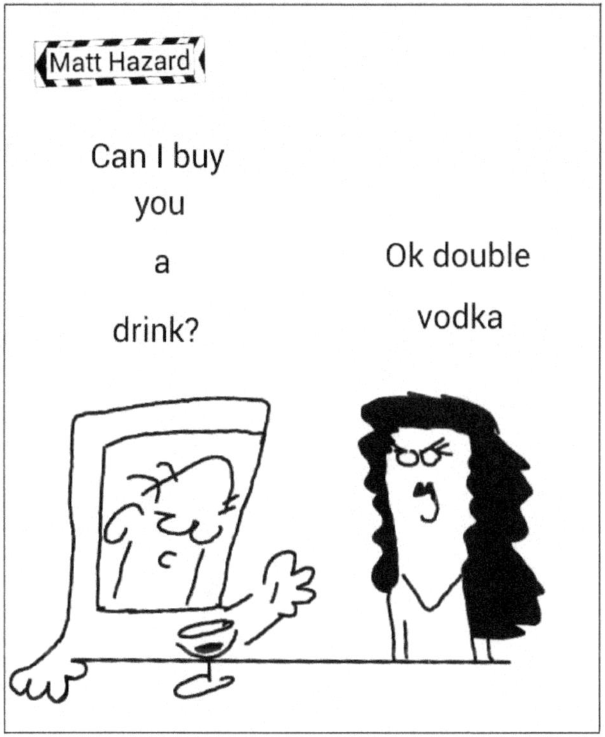
Matt Hazard
Can I buy you a drink?
Ok double vodka

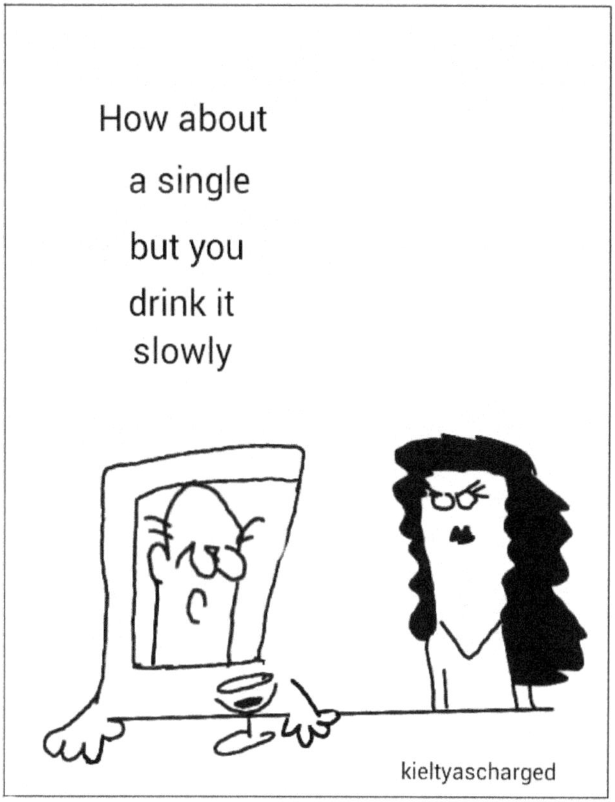
How about a single but you drink it slowly
kieltyascharged

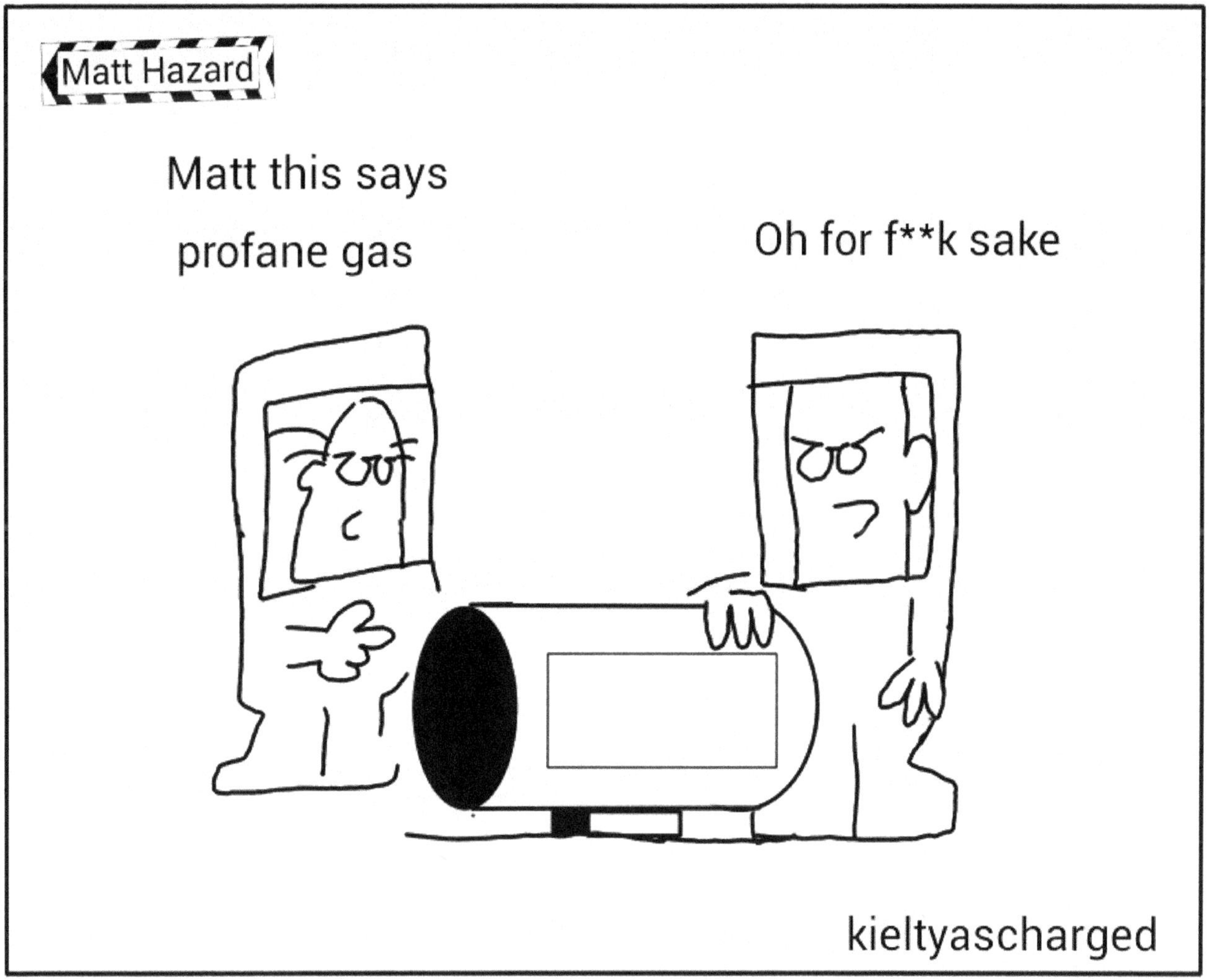
Matt Hazard
Matt this says
profane gas
Oh for f**k sake
kieltyascharged

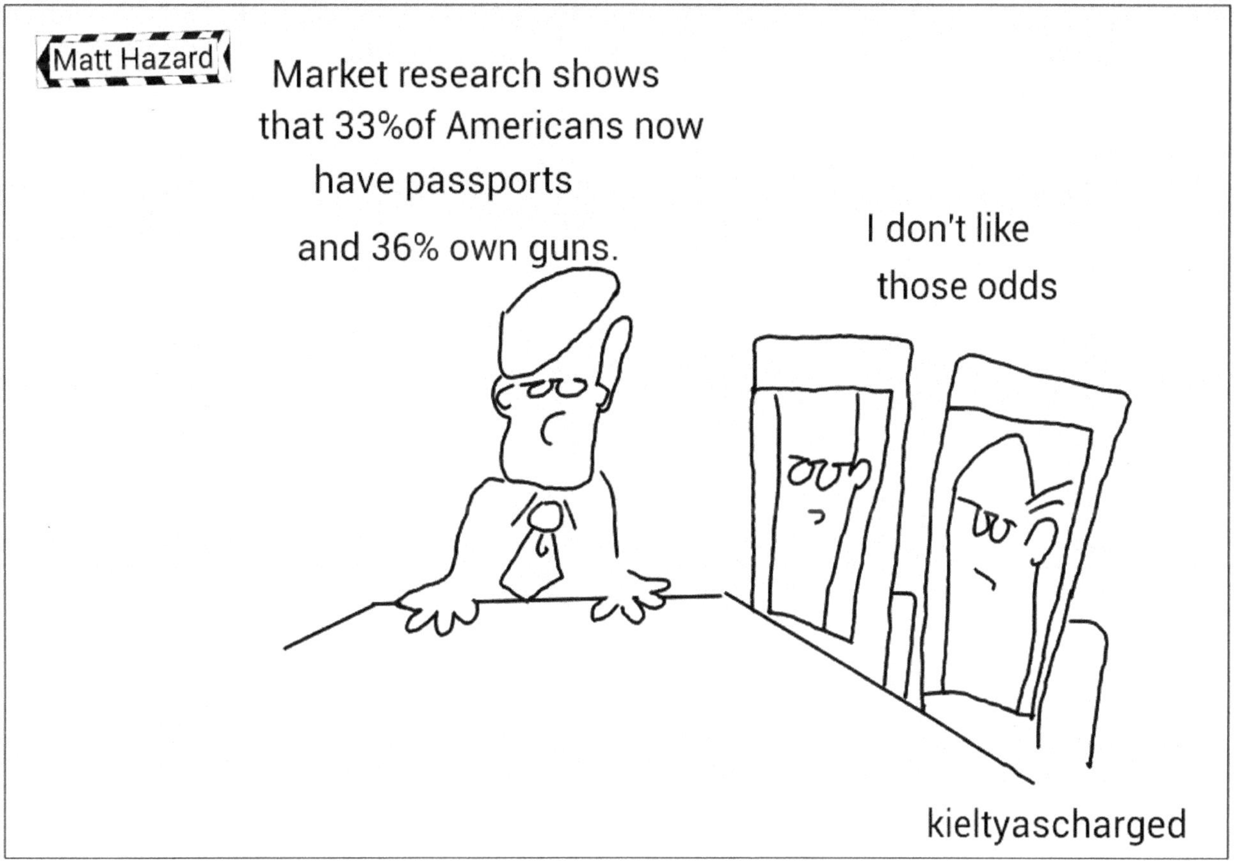
Matt Hazard
Market research shows that 33%of Americans now have passports
and 36% own guns.
I don't like those odds
kieltyascharged

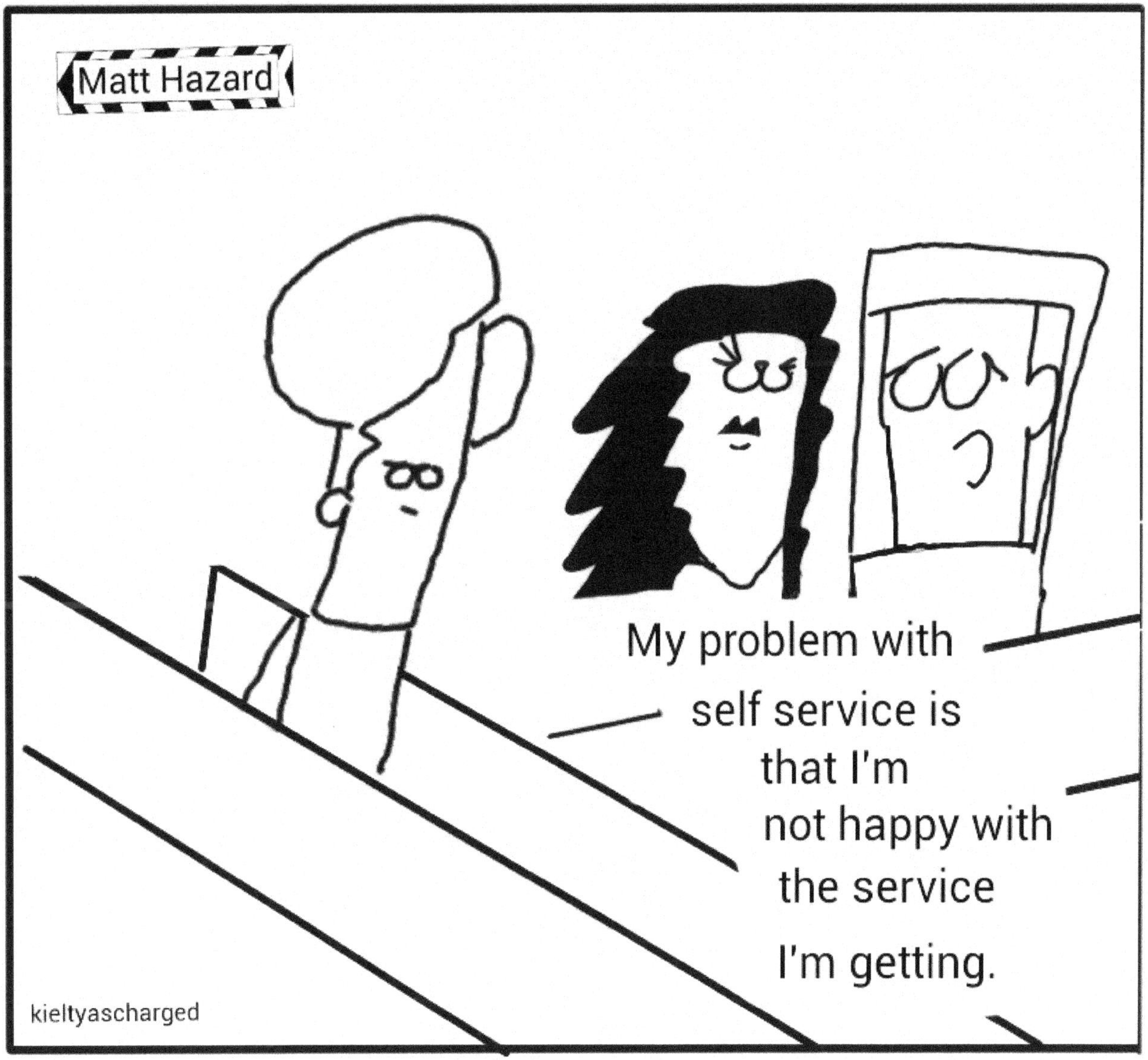
Matt Hazard
My problem with self service is that I'm not happy with the service I'm getting.
kieltyascharged

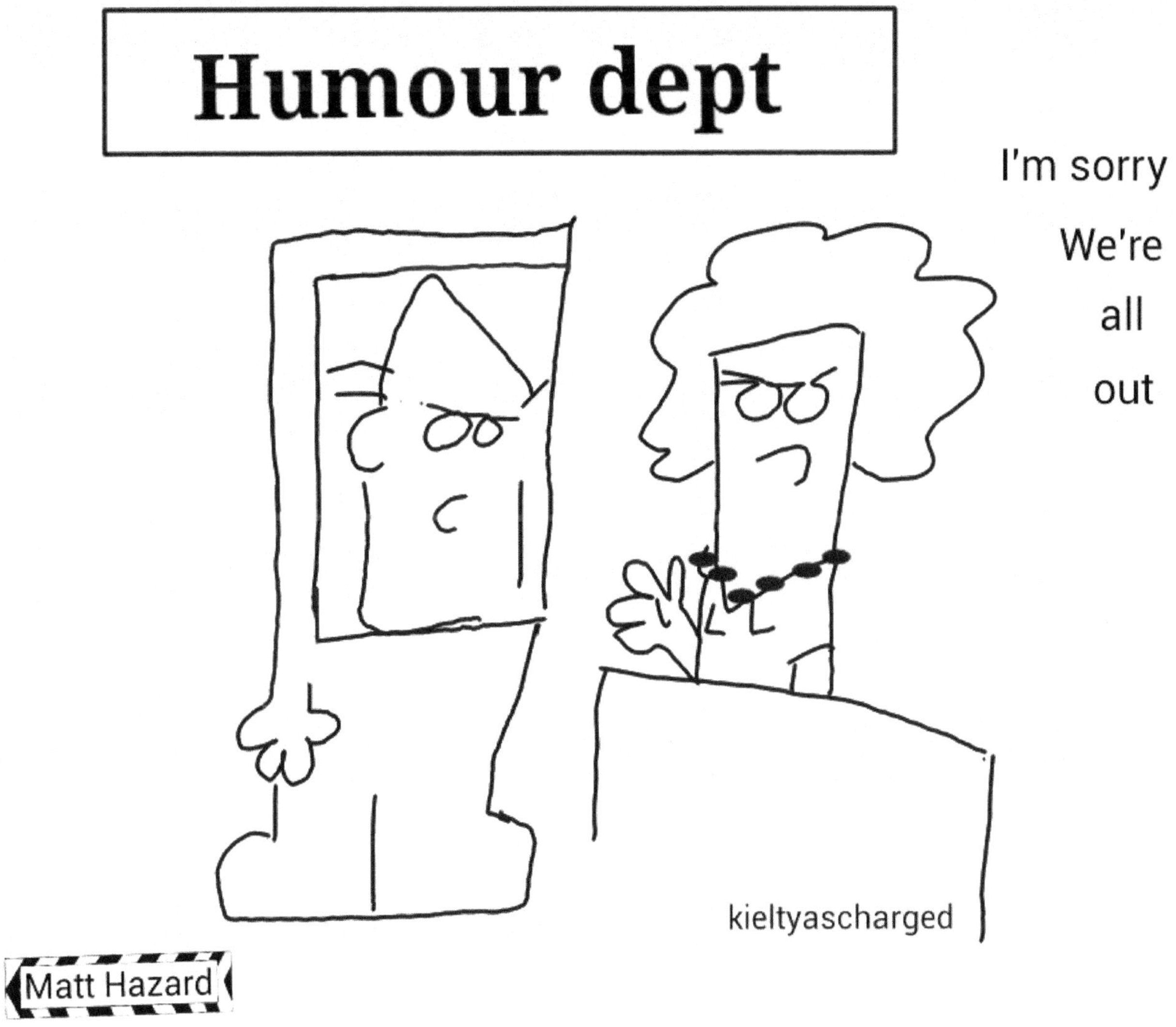
Humour dept
I'm sorry
We're
all
out
kieltyascharged
Matt Hazard

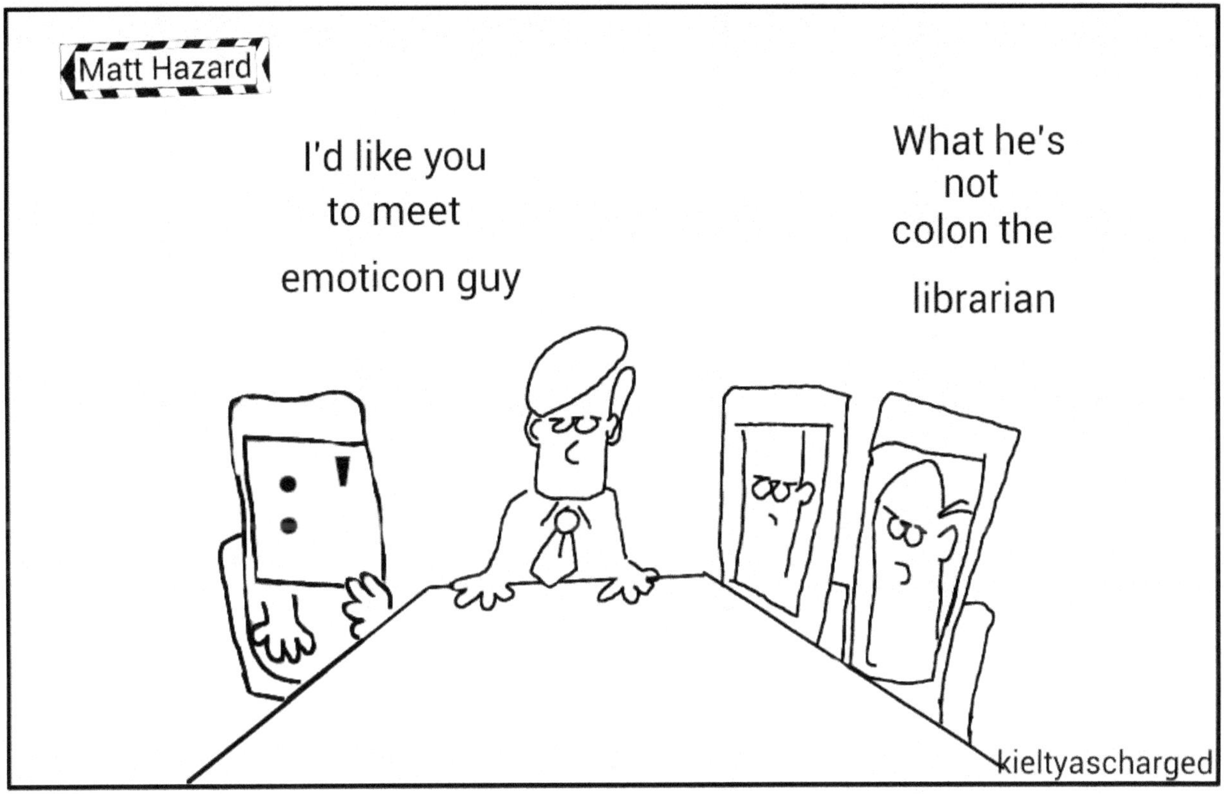
Matt Hazard
I'd like you to meet emoticon guy
What he's not colon the librarian
kieltyascharged

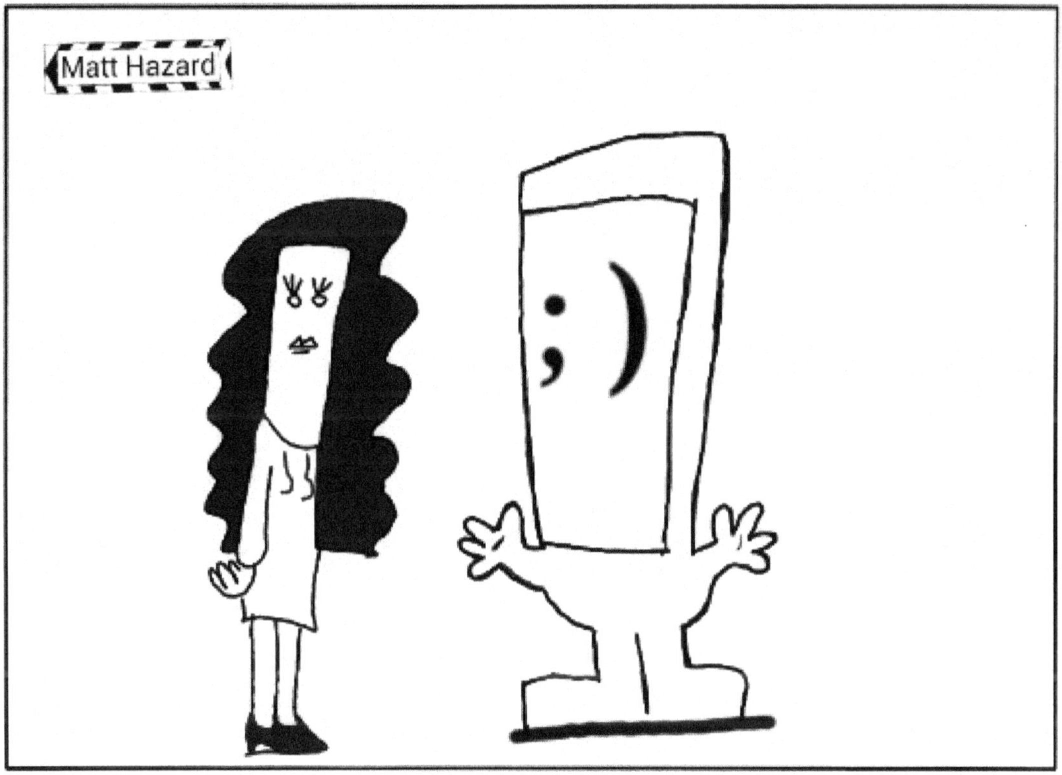
Matt Hazard

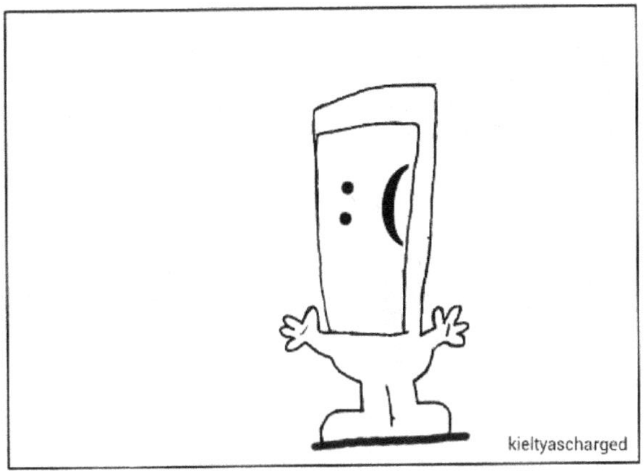
kieltyascharged

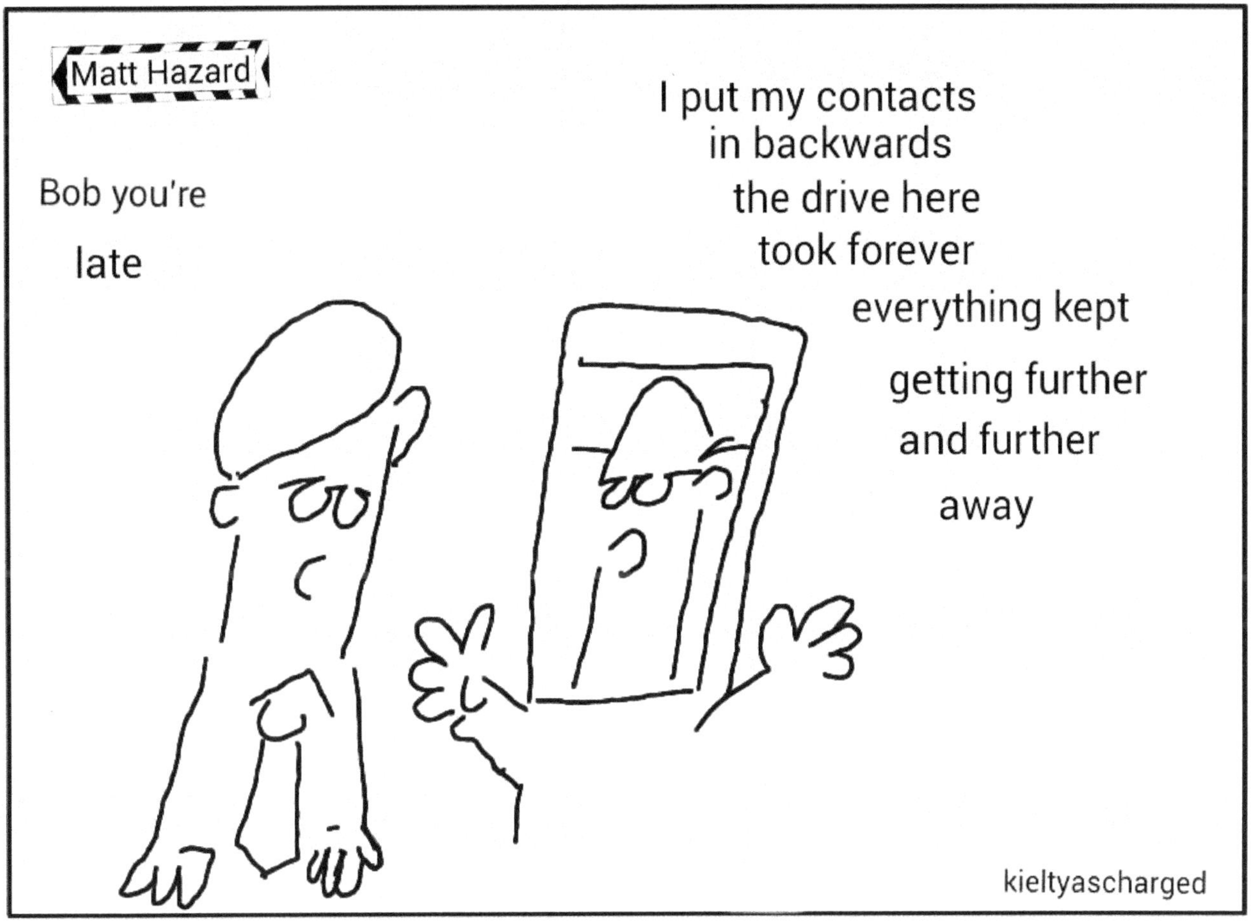
Matt Hazard
Bob you're
late
I put my contacts
in backwards
the drive here
took forever
everything kept
getting further
and further
away
kieltyascharged

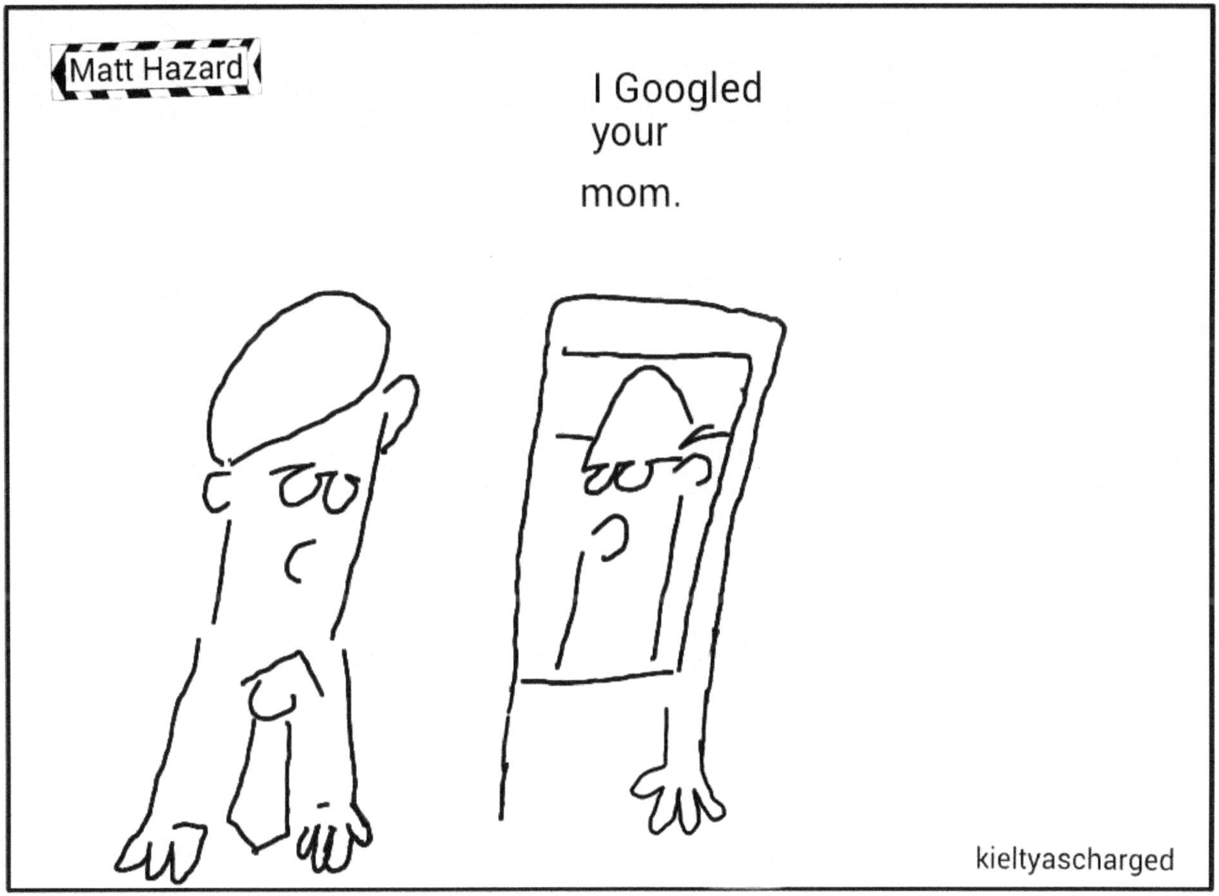
Matt Hazard
I Googled your mom.
kieltyascharged

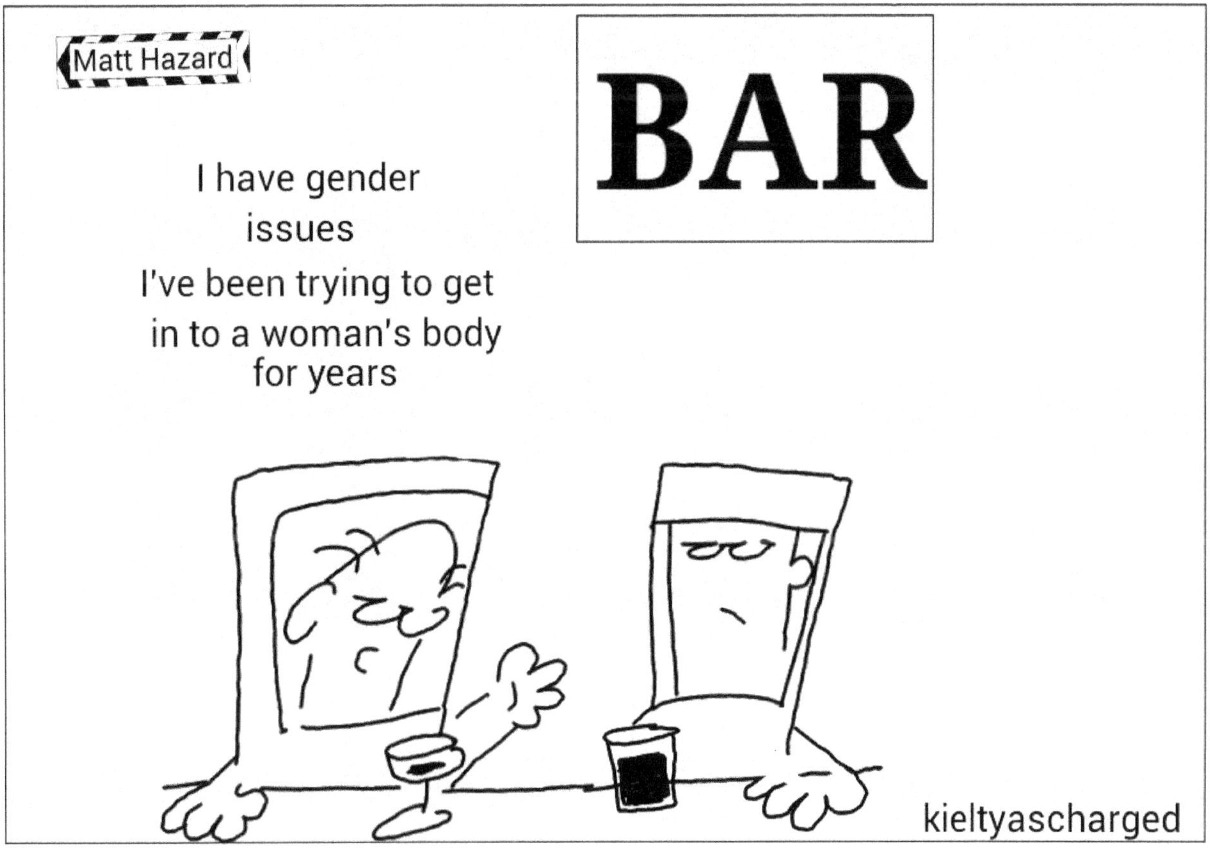
Matt Hazard
BAR
I have gender issues
I've been trying to get in to a woman's body for years
kieltyascharged

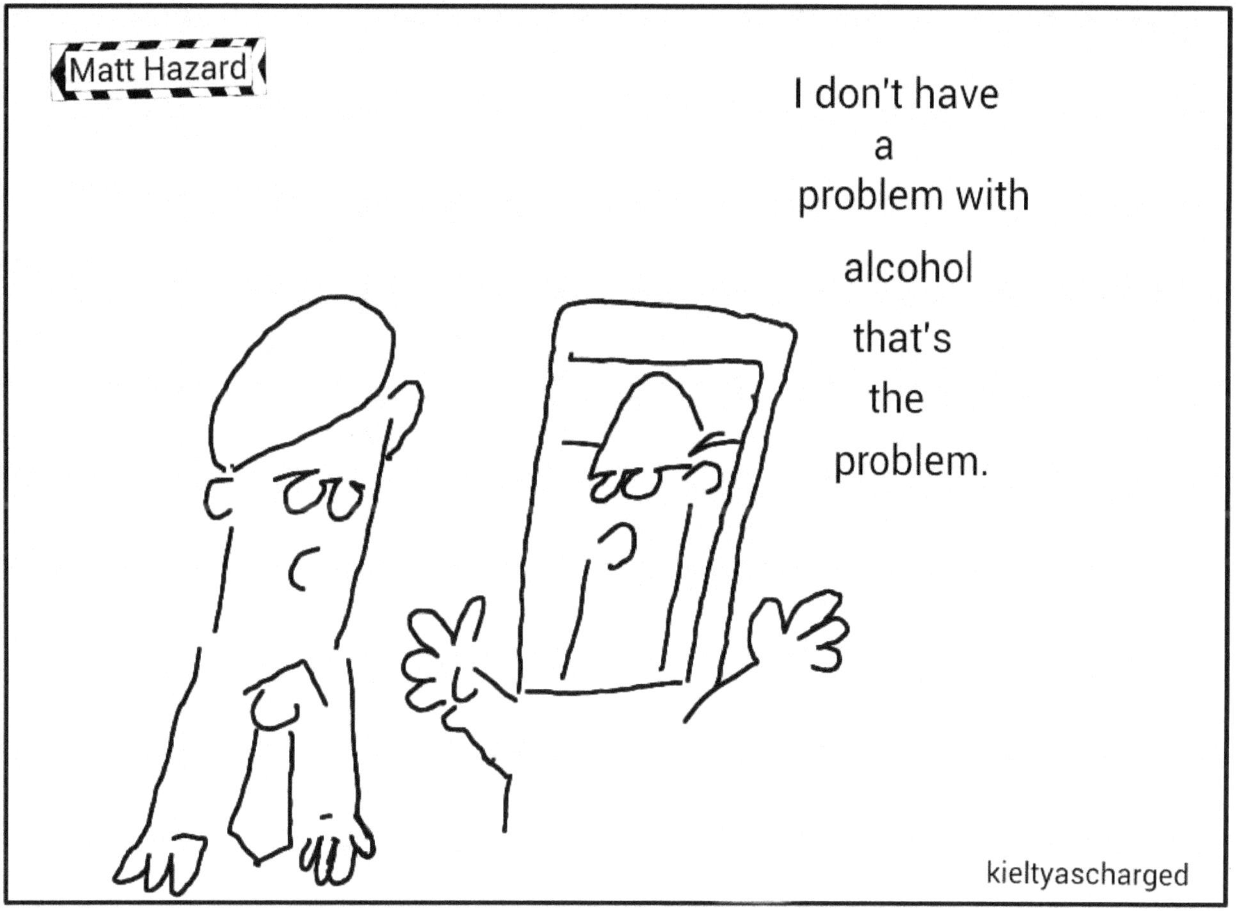
Matt Hazard
I don't have a problem with alcohol that's the problem.
kieltyascharged

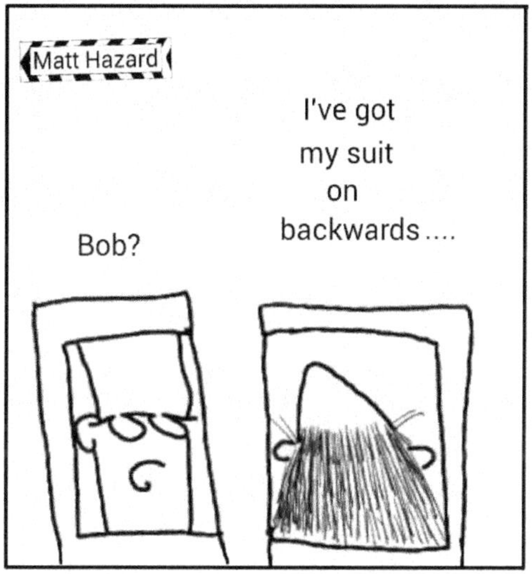
Matt Hazard
Bob?
I've got my suit on backwards....

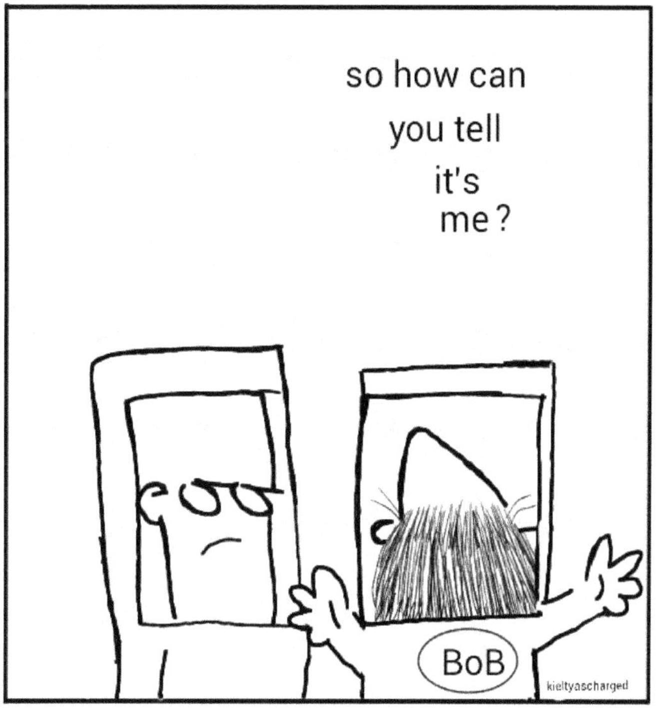
so how can you tell it's me?
BoB
kieltyascharged

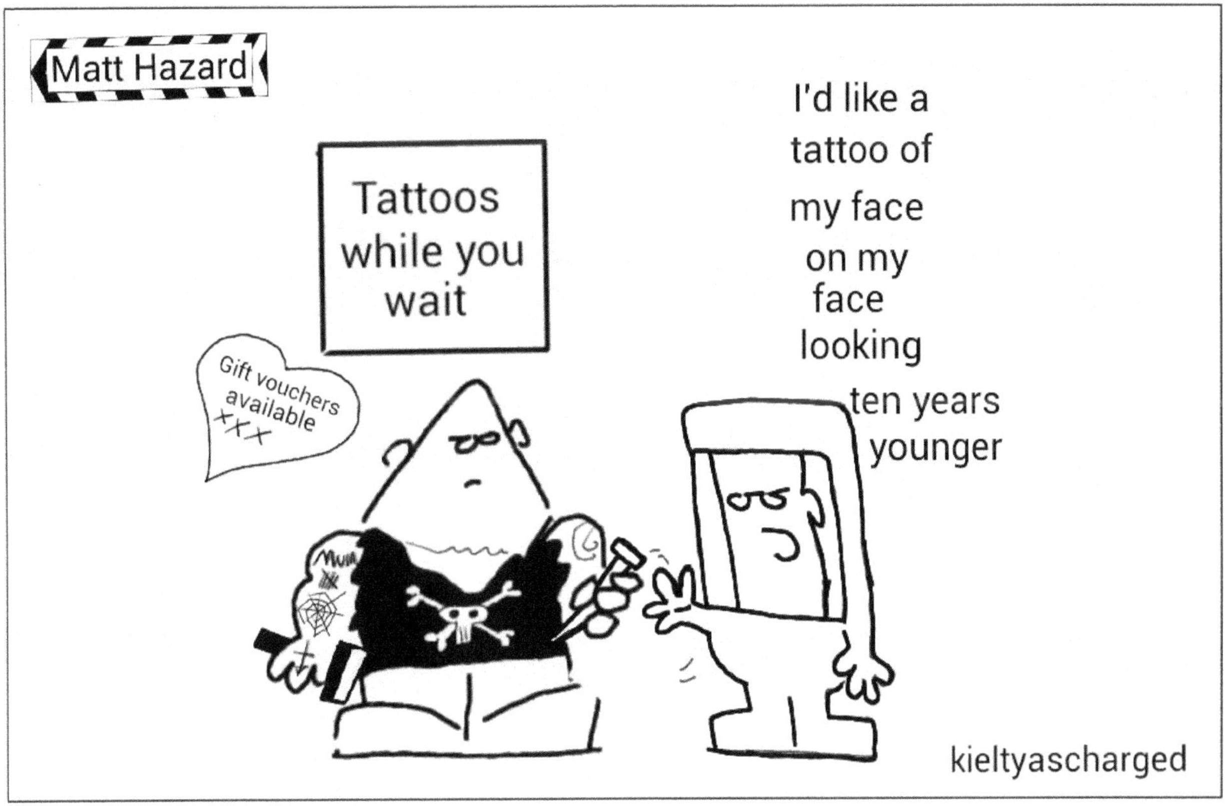
Matt Hazard
Tattoos while you wait
Gift vouchers available xxx
I'd like a tattoo of my face on my face looking ten years younger
kieltyascharged

Matt Hazard

Listen the
birds are
tweeting.

That's because
they're
on line

kieltyascharged

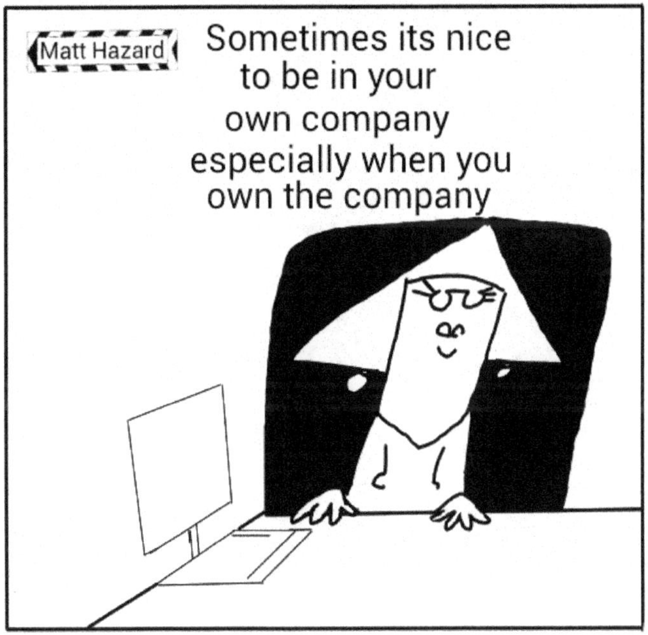
Matt Hazard
Sometimes its nice to be in your own company especially when you own the company

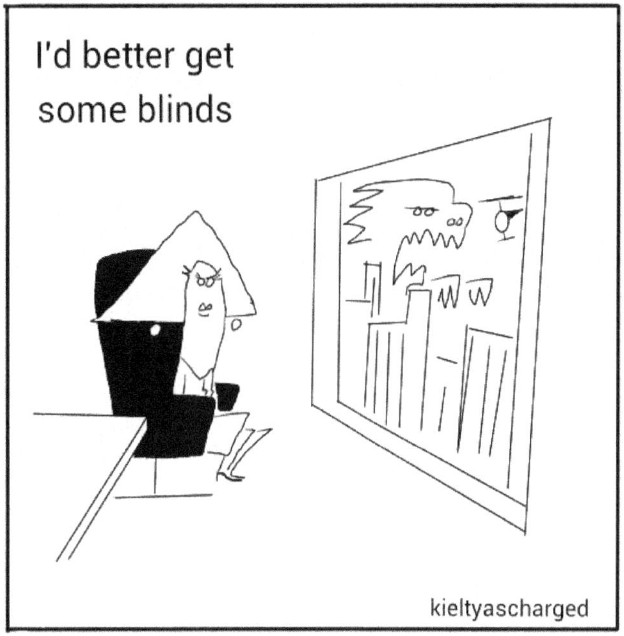
I'd better get some blinds
kieltyascharged

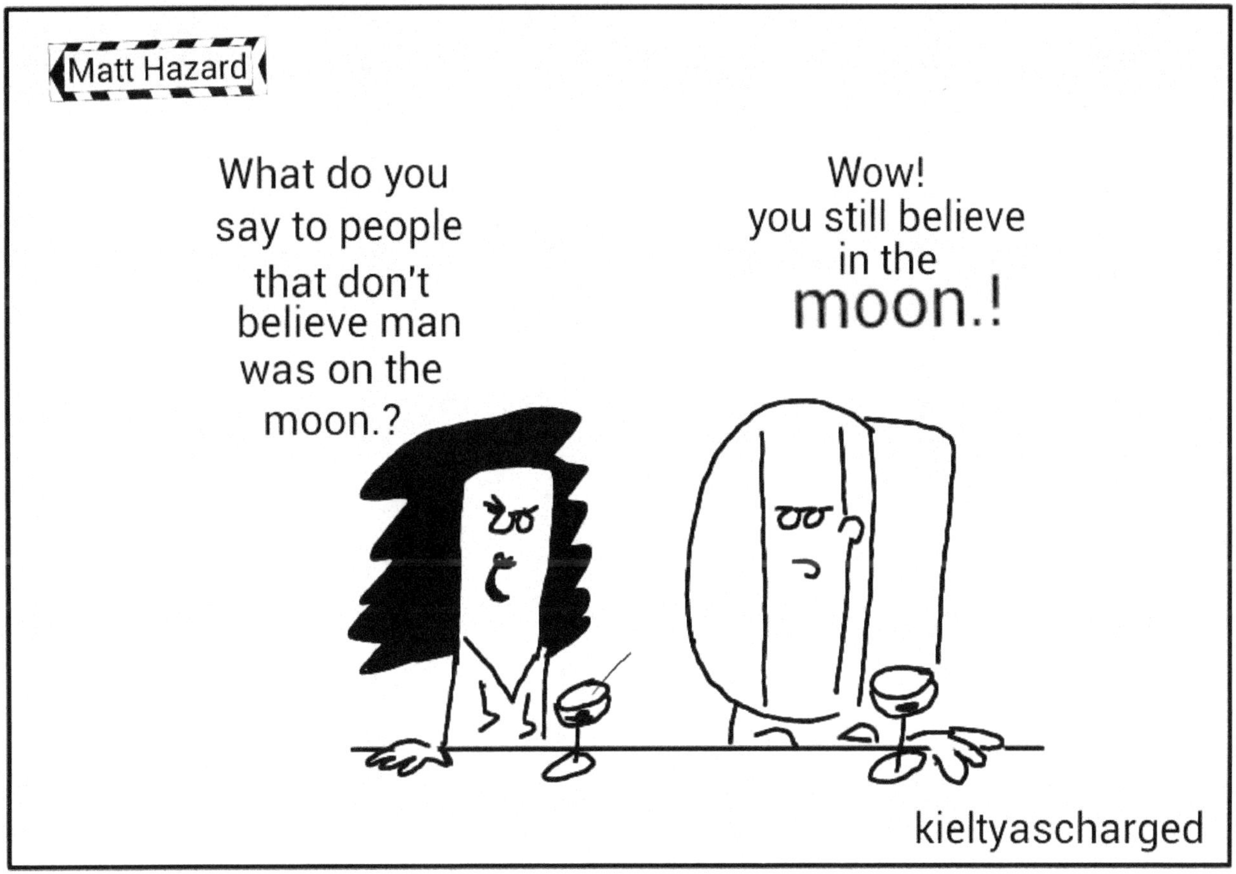
Matt Hazard
What do you say to people that don't believe man was on the moon.?
Wow! you still believe in the moon.!
kieltyascharged

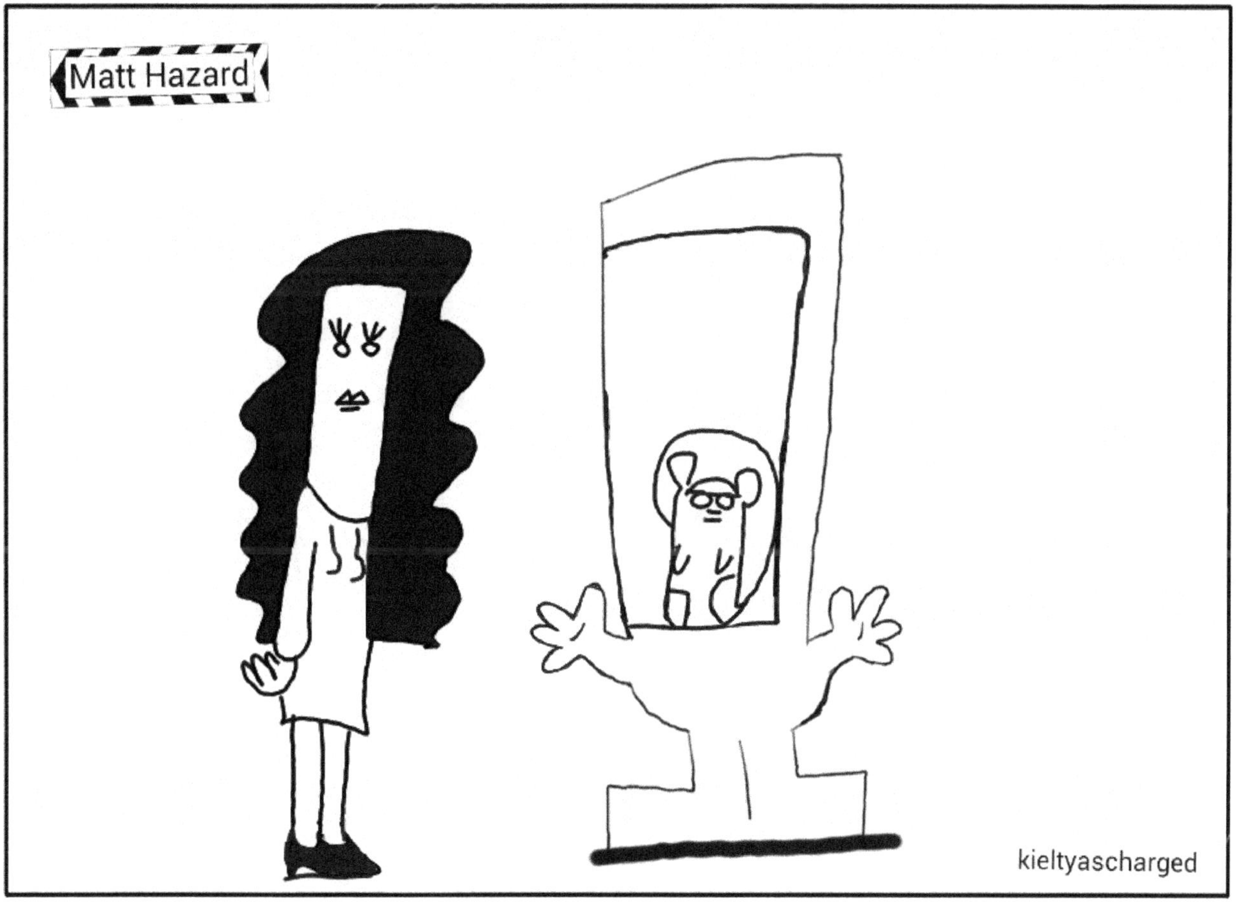
Matt Hazard
kieltyascharged

Matt Hazard

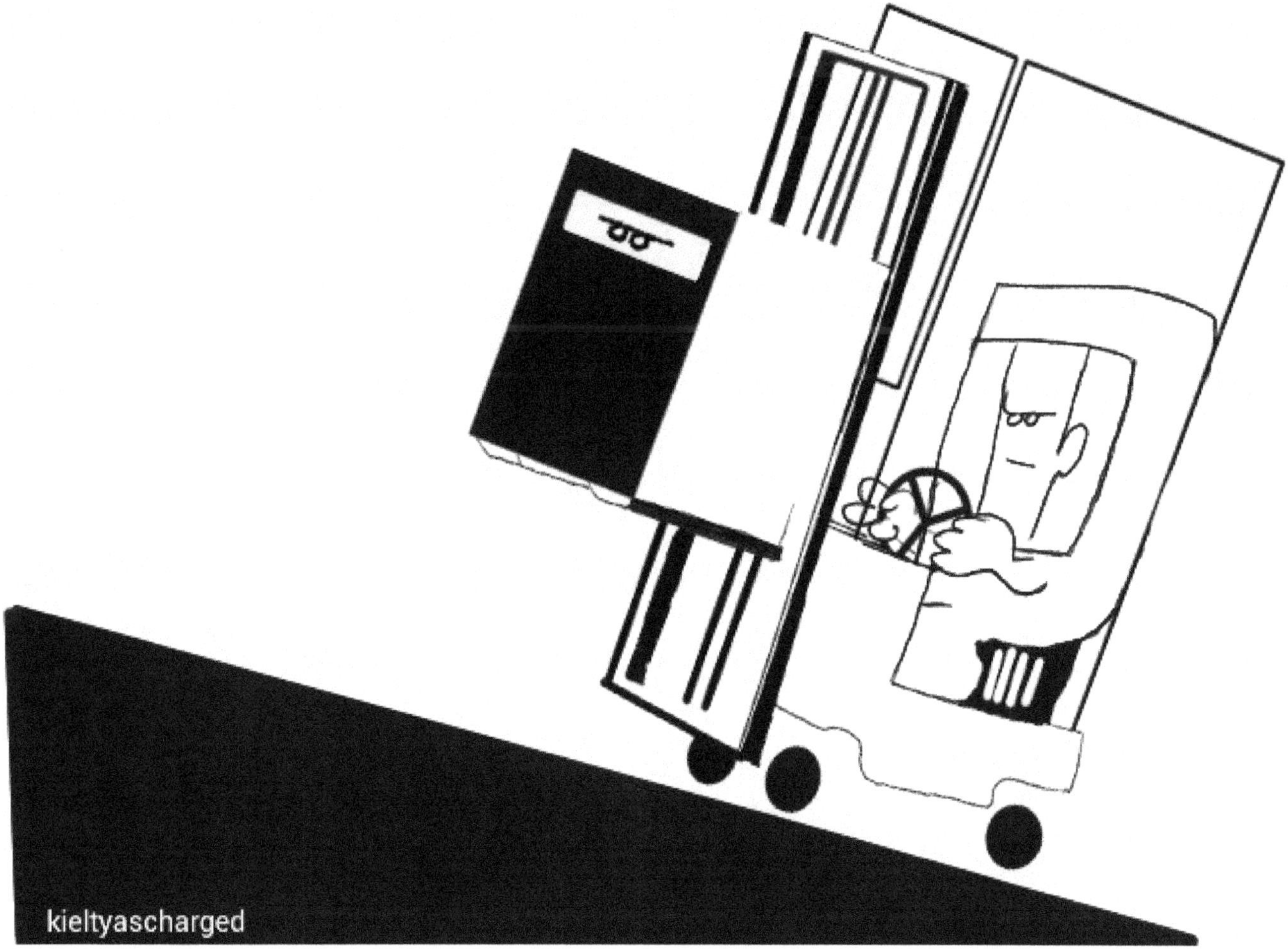
kieltyascharged

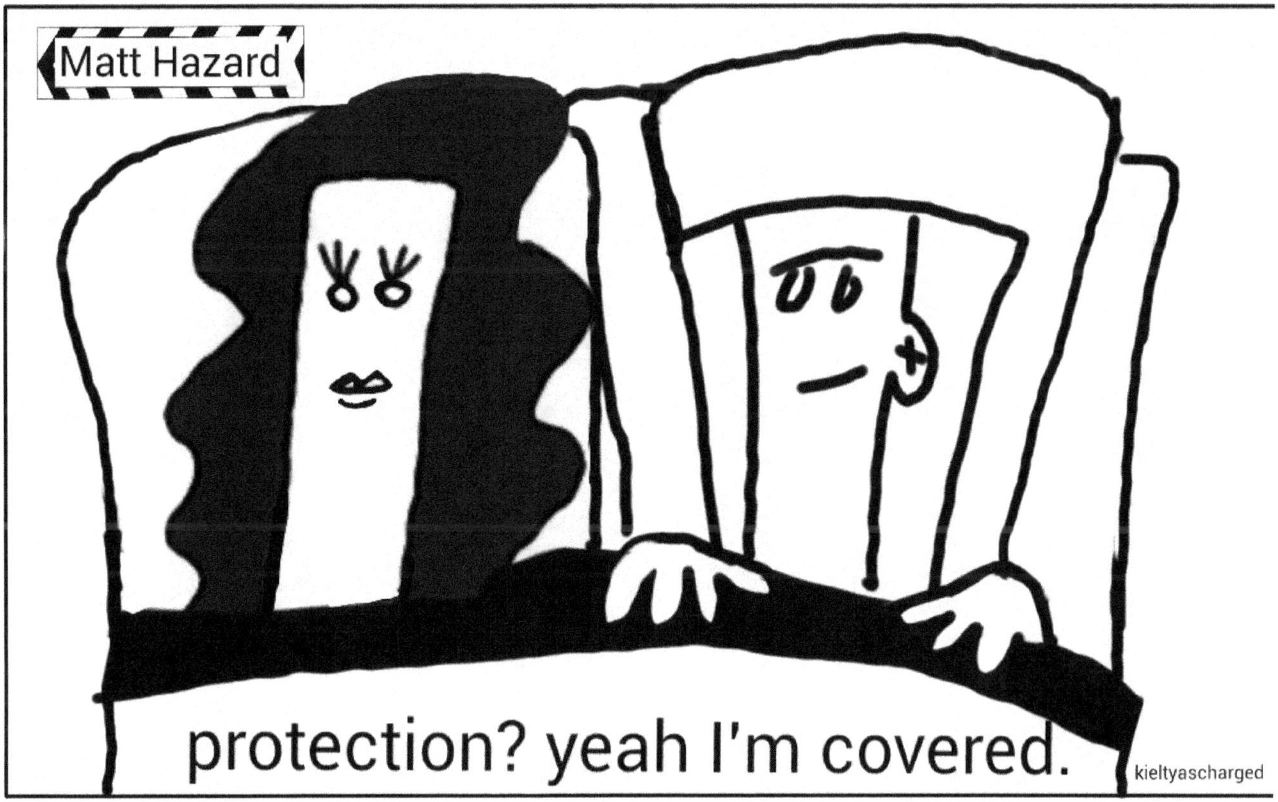
Matt Hazard
protection? yeah I'm covered.
kieltyascharged

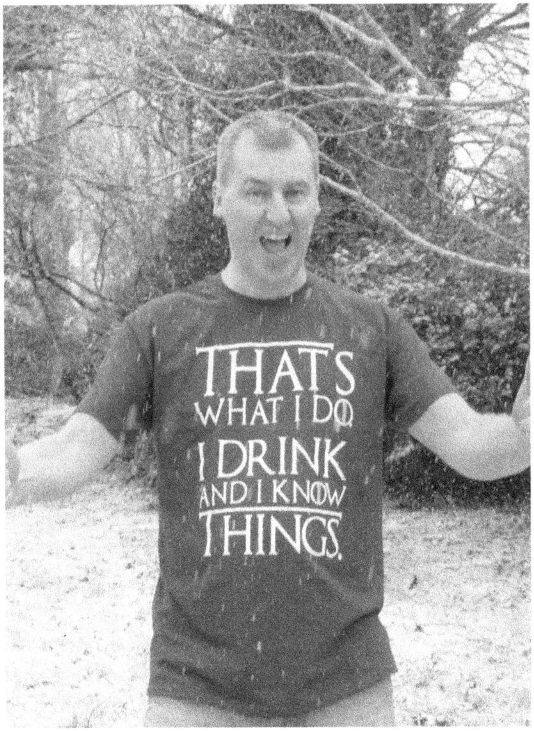
THATS
WHAT I DO
I DRINK
AND I KNOW
THINGS.

Paul "kieltyascharged" Kielty is an Irishman living in the midlands of England. No wonder he has an odd slant on life…

Paul worked for many years, first on the factory floor, then rising to the dizzying heights of foreman before jacking it all in to follow every Irishman's dream – to leave their beloved country.

His excuse was that he was offered an animation degree at the University of Wolverhampton. He started an M.A. but holding 2 jobs down (Animation technician and warehousing) to pay the rent and university fees finally meant he took up warehousing/ labouring/ factory work full time, once more:
though always dabbling in Stand-up comedy, M.C.-ing at burlesque nights, singer-songwriting and recording, drawing, painting, and developing his origami skills in his spare time.

2018 sees him "coming out" as an artist – with this, his first book of MATTOONS – and a high-end visual art exhibition.

His friends and enemies alike tend to sum him up as a man who drinks beer and knows things…

So he got himself the t-shirt

www.ingramcontent.com/pod-product-compliance
Lightning Source LLC
LaVergne TN
LVHW081324060426
835511LV00011B/1837